Lean for the Public Sector

The Pursuit of Perfection in Government Services

D1342465

Lean for the Public Sector

The Pursuit of Perfection in Government Services

BERT TEEUWEN

CRC Press
Taylor & Francis Group
Boca Raton London New York

CRC Press is an imprint of the
Taylor & Francis Group, an **informa** business

A PRODUCTIVITY PRESS BOOK

Productivity Press
Taylor & Francis Group
270 Madison Avenue
New York, NY 10016

© 2011 by Taylor and Francis Group, LLC
Productivity Press is an imprint of Taylor & Francis Group, an Informa business

No claim to original U.S. Government works

Printed in the United States of America on acid-free paper
10 9 8 7 6 5 4 3 2 1

International Standard Book Number: 978-1-4398-4022-1 (Paperback)

This book contains information obtained from authentic and highly regarded sources. Reasonable efforts have been made to publish reliable data and information, but the author and publisher cannot assume responsibility for the validity of all materials or the consequences of their use. The authors and publishers have attempted to trace the copyright holders of all material reproduced in this publication and apologize to copyright holders if permission to publish in this form has not been obtained. If any copyright material has not been acknowledged please write and let us know so we may rectify in any future reprint.

Except as permitted under U.S. Copyright Law, no part of this book may be reprinted, reproduced, transmitted, or utilized in any form by any electronic, mechanical, or other means, now known or hereafter invented, including photocopying, microfilming, and recording, or in any information storage or retrieval system, without written permission from the publishers.

For permission to photocopy or use material electronically from this work, please access www.copyright.com (http://www.copyright.com/) or contact the Copyright Clearance Center, Inc. (CCC), 222 Rosewood Drive, Danvers, MA 01923, 978-750-8400. CCC is a not-for-profit organization that provides licenses and registration for a variety of users. For organizations that have been granted a photocopy license by the CCC, a separate system of payment has been arranged.

Trademark Notice: Product or corporate names may be trademarks or registered trademarks, and are used only for identification and explanation without intent to infringe.

Library of Congress Cataloging-in-Publication Data

Teeuwen, Bert.
   [Procesgericht verbeteren in de Publieke Sector. English]
   Lean for the public sector : the pursuit of perfection in government services / Bert Teeuwen.
      p. cm.
   Includes bibliographical references and index.
   ISBN 978-1-4398-4022-1
   1. Government productivity. 2. Government productivity--Measurement. 3. Administrative agencies--Reorganization. 4. Executive departments--Reorganization. I. Title.

JF1525.P67T4413 2010
352.3'4--dc22
                                                                          2010020740

Visit the Taylor & Francis Web site at
http://www.taylorandfrancis.com

and the Productivity Press Web site at
http://www.productivitypress.com

Contents

Preface

Can you run a public organization as an enterprise? Where the customer is king?

There is a movement in the public sector to recognize individuals as government customers. This relationship suggests that the public may expect the best from its government and it only has to wait for this to happen. Consumerism in the public sector has changed the language in town halls and other places where individuals interact with the government. Individuals are seen as customers buying products from the government, and the government is customer-oriented and serves customers in its shops. The positive effect is that governments spent more time increasing the quality of service. The negative effect is the creation of a customer mentality in which citizens do not feel responsible anymore for their own neighborhoods. They behave like customers: passive and demanding.

The public sector embraces the principles of modern management and market processes and is concerned with management and with guiding the development of society. This occurs at every level of society, from precinct, municipality, county, state, and nation to international organizations, such as the United Nations and NATO. However, the government is not alone in this. To address social problems and guide society in the right direction, other players, such as businesses, individuals, and social organizations, must be included. These players are not passive, nameless consumers; they have an active role to play and a personal responsibility. They are more than mere customers. Many individuals have little desire for the government to start acting as a supplier. Extensive research has shown that individuals, with regard to services, consider the most important traits of an effective government to be: reachability, accessibility, timing (accurate and fast), and personal attention/input. Individuals value not only the services they receive but also the attention, plus the possibility of personal input. With regard to efficiency, individuals have requested that the government not waste tax money, but do something useful with it.

I Don't Make the Rules

This doesn't mean that there isn't room for improvement in public services. Today, processes in the public sector are based on the principles of integrity, equality, and controllability. In most cases, these principles were drawn from the policies, legislation, and the efficiency of the internal organization, with justification and control more strongly in mind than the request for assistance. For example, if communication with the public becomes difficult, a public servant may say that he/she doesn't make the rules and, thus, the individual is no longer the focus. At many local government offices, a line is drawn on the floor that asks clients to wait *behind* this line, in essence for the respect and privacy of other clients. Please note that this has been written from the perspective of the public servant *behind* the counter, and that the customer, in fact, is required to wait *before* the line. Place yourself in the individual's position. From the civil servant's point of view, there is nothing wrong with the idea of a citizen customer, as the government's image is generally poor, and there is much that can be improved upon in terms of service. It is also prudent to learn the best practices from the private sector, because these practices can be made to fit the public sector.

A practice of the private sector that may be successfully adopted in the public sector is the Lean Improvement Program. Lean is a management philosophy aimed at maximizing value for the customer and eliminating *waste*—activities that have no added value. This method originated in the automotive industry. Lean production improves the quality of products and services and cuts back costs, which improves business results.

It is of the utmost importance not to consider Lean as a set of smart tools that improve processes or cut back costs. Lean is a way of thinking, an attitude. Lean for the public sector means putting the individual center stage, not the public servant or politics. With Lean for the Public Sector, employees who work for governmental organizations are constantly looking to eliminate waste. The attitude of the executives is aimed at making employees the owner of the processes. They set targets and criteria but offer no solutions.

How This Book Is Organized

This book is about Lean Management; however, in our case, it is for the *public* sector. The cases and examples come from a variety of countries. Because every country has its own vision of public services, the processes mentioned in this book may not be the same as in the country in which you live. Nevertheless, the citizen-oriented attitude and the use of the Lean tools are applicable for all public organizations in free countries.

The chapters in this book cover the following subjects:

Chapter 1. *Introduction to Lean Management*

How does improvement take place in most of the traditional public organizations? What are the differences between provision of services by organizations in the business sector and the public sector? What is Lean Management and what are its basic principles? Keywords include: improvement management, five stages of Lean.

Chapter 2. *Adding Value: Who Is the Customer?*

Businesses have customers, how about the government? Individuals are always changing roles. The seven roles of individuals are explained by way of examples. Lean distinguishes between value-adding activities and waste. When does the government add value in terms of the different roles of individuals? Keywords include: add value, the seven roles of the individual, quality parameters.

Chapter 3. *Determine Value*

Processes are composed of value-adding activities and wastes. There are eight so-called "deadly wastes" in public processes. In these processes, we discriminate between lead time and action time. Individuals often play an active role in these processes, which is sometimes considered desirable and at other times burdensome. Keywords include: the eight deadly wastes, action time, lead time, integrity, and efficiency.

Chapter 4. *Mapping the Value Stream*

Administrative processes are reasonably invisible because they are hidden inside people's heads, in computers, and in documents. The value stream of a process can be made visible with the help of a value stream analysis. However, we must first address a few basic questions, such as: Is the process necessary at all? Keywords include: value stream analysis, current state, future state.

Chapter 5. *Flow and the Pull Principle*

Processes should run smoothly. In Lean jargon, this is called flow. A process with flow features has little or no stock or checks and runs at a rate adjusted to the customer's demand. The public pulls the process—the pull principle. However, in the public sector, the push principle is sometimes better. Keywords include: one-piece flow, Takt time, pull and push principles, line balancing, working cells, con WIP.

Chapter 6. *Mobilize Employees*

Employees working on processes each day are process experts. They know how the processes run in practice and how individuals react in real life. Are you, the executive, ignoring this? Are you designing your own processes? Are you having an external consultant do it? Improving processes is fun. People enjoy doing it. Mobilize your workforce and have them participate in kaizen teams. Keywords: kaizen teams, ownership, enjoying the work, the organization of Lean, sustaining Lean, everyday Lean.

Chapter 7. *Continuous Improvement with Kaizen Teams*

W. Edwards Deming PlanDoCheckAct (PDCA) improvement circle is a powerful instrument for every improvement step. In this chapter, PDCA is divided over eight steps. We explain the eight-step circle by means of an example: a kaizen event at the social services. Keywords include: PDCA, kaizen event, 5×Why

Chapter 8. *Standardization and Compliance*

The word standardize brings to mind images of work instructions and procedures. Yet, these standards are not very strong. There are better ways of securing processes and preventing mistakes. Keywords: compliance pyramid, fail safes, poka-yoke, one-point lessons

Chapter 9. *The Perfect Public Service Provider*

Starting Lean is not difficult, but how does one keep the improvement wheel turning? For example, how does one control deadly wastes every day, with the individual center stage set. What does the ideal public service provider look like? What results can be achieved with Lean? A list of results from real-life situations and two examples of simple solutions with a serious impact on the process are discussed in this chapter. How do politicians relate to Lean? Keywords include: the ideal, improvement board, lean organization, instrumentalists.

Chapter 10. *The Process-Oriented Organization*

Government organizations that merge or cooperate often reorganize the traditional way. The reorganization is from within; all kinds of issues, such as strategic targets, organizational charts, the layout of the building, formation plans, and job descriptions have been settled before the processes are designed. The result is processes designed to meet efficiency, not the public's demands. Keywords include: Lean and reorganizing/merging, task-oriented or process-oriented organization, vertical start-up.

Chapter 11. *Lean and Cost Savings*

Governmental organizations must make cutbacks from time to time.

A leaner organization doesn't always sound very attractive. There are several views on cutbacks, such as less for less and more for less. Is it possible to connect Lean to cutbacks? Even when you're not cutting back, what do you do with the time you gain with Lean? Keywords include: add value, cutback, capitalize.

Chapter 12. *Workplace Organization Based on the 5Ss*

A messy desk is a messy head, the famous Italian educationalist Maria Montessori would say. In our case, if the environment is messy or even chaotic, the processes will have that same quality. 5S workspace organization is a powerful instrument to organize and visualize the workspace. Keywords include: 30-second rule, 5S, clean desk, digital 5S.

Purpose of This Book

This is a how-to workbook that helps you to immediately integrate the Lean way of thinking and its tools into your improvement program. It provides enough means for managing the entire Lean transformation progress in your public organization. The purpose of this book is to:

■ Adapt Lean thinking and tools to the public sector.
■ Demonstrate that Lean in the public sector is neither rocket science nor a typical profit-driven improvement program.
■ Give enough basic principles and tools to start with Lean in your own public organization.

It is possible you have met English-speaking consultants who suddenly started talking Japanese to you (Figure FM.1); using words like *jidoka, heijunka, muri, muda,* and so on. Quite possibly these were instrumentalists who consider Lean a set of handy tools. Keep in mind that it's not the tools, it's the attitude!

Enjoy your reading.

Bert Teeuwen

I understand your problem. I suggest we first eliminate the 研究社 with the application of 工作機械, 道具箱 and 輸送する. After that, the 掃除 should be 養う with the combination of 平ら 水平 にすること and たわごと. By the way, did I tell you that I visited a Toyota plant in Japan? The next step will be a 価値 流れ 地図作成 — training, followed by the implementation of 価値 流れ 地図作成. Things like 時に and 具体的には will likely motivate your people...

© B. Teeuwen

The consultant explains the road to success...

Acknowledgments

I would like to express my gratitude to all who made the writing of this book possible, in particular Klaas Verboom and Twan Kersten for their valuable insights and recommendations and Arri Hartog (Drechtsteden Tax) and Dick Vollbehr (head of Social Services for the Oldambt Council) for their cooperation and input on the real-life cases described in this book. I am also grateful to Michael Sinocchi of Productivity Press, who accepted this work.

Chapter 1

Introduction to Lean Management

The term *improvement management* stands for the way in which improvements are implemented inside an organization. It is the subject of much discussion in the industry, and reams and reams of publications have been devoted to it. In the public sector, improvement management is on the rise, although it has not yet received the attention required to improve its image and to make it more effective for the public.

Individuals, on the whole, do not hold a positive view of the performance of public services. Strike up a conversation about government at any party and see what happens. Everyone has something to say on the subject, and you will be flooded with examples of lingering bureaucracy and obscure official lingo. The image the government projects in the area of services is not much to write home about.

Of course, the public sector has the drawback of being public—because, let's be fair, the world of business, too, is riddled with depressingly poor service. Critical consumer programs on television only show the tip of the iceberg, and if you are a member of a consumer organization, you are kept abreast of company failures. Try to terminate your membership with an Internet provider, change your insurance company, or get hooked up with an ADSL (asymmetric digital subscriber line). Even a death certificate does not stop some companies from continuing to send advertising, bills, and reminders.

What does not help the situation is that individuals are forced to purchase mandatory products from a monopolist government. On top of this, these products are not delivered quickly and clearly, and it can get frustrating very quickly. Some would argue that the government, as a provider of public services, is a necessary evil at best—one you can only hope will trouble you as little as possible. In some countries, the government has focused on reducing the administrative burden for individuals and businesses. In fact, the message that is conveyed is that it is a burden, but the government will try to make it as painless as possible, which is a negative attitude. The individuals, in addition to being relieved of some of their burden, also should profit from the government, for example by means of a joint development from which both individuals and the government can benefit. Another concern is how the public's tax money is spent. Individuals like the idea of a maximum return on sensible projects achieved with a minimum of their tax money. It is only right that they take a hard look at how the government spends their tax money.

Improvement in the Public Sector

The government must implement improvement initiatives in order to rid itself of its bad image. Programs for relieving the administrative burden for individuals and businesses and professionalizing services are attempts to get the local governments moving. There are subsidies for councils and counties that can demonstrate success, and there are also public organizations that have started creating quality standards for their services. There is little improvement so far, but there is a greater focus on the public's needs. Below are some quotes on service standards from municipal quality manifests (2008):

> *You can apply for a wheelchair if you are dependent on a daily basis. We will decide on your application within four months.*
>
> *We (Council S) guarantee the following about the products mentioned here. Decision on an application for handicapped parking: eight weeks.*
>
> *We will attend to your letter within two weeks. If this is impossible, we will send you a progress report—Council A, USA.*
>
> *We will answer the telephone within 20 seconds of ringing (7 rings)—Council of a London Borough, U.K.*
>
> *Calls will be answered in a courteous manner (with a smile)— City of R/Maryland, USA.*
>
> *The city of C, Australia, replies to letters and e-mail concerning street lighting enquiries within 28 days.*

Figure 1.1

The service standards in these quality manifests are occasionally stricter than the legal terms, but then there is no shame in aiming a little higher.

In times of economic crisis, the state forces local authorities to cut back. Cutbacks, which are ultimately paid for by the public through increased taxation or by cutting subsidies and other services, are not the sort of measures that individuals have in mind when hoping for less regulation and fewer public servants (Figure 1.1).

These examples all begin with political and societal pressure. In the end, they are all top-down initiatives. Do local authorities ever make a move themselves? They do occasionally, but what is missing is that local government does not feel the need to improve. Individuals cannot switch to the competition, and public organizations cannot collapse as a result of bankruptcy. It is important to have competition because it stimulates the need to constantly improve. If you do not do it right, you lose. The German fashion designer Karl Lagerfeld put it this way, "Competition is healthy, you know. Some people would like the idea of no competition, so they can keep the position for the rest of their lives, but no, there has to be a kind of danger all the time. I think it's very healthy, it makes you better." (CNN, December 2009).

Some public services have broken away and have embraced an improvement program that truly targets better and cheaper services. In addition, initiatives do develop after listening to individuals and businesses. The products and the organizations are not center stage; rather, it is the public's needs and requirements. Process lead times are cut by a minimum of 50%.

Wait times are minimized and documents are short and readable, and services go beyond simply meeting legal standards and periods.

Improvement management in the public sector is about doing more with less and adding more value for individuals and businesses with less time and money for the organization itself and less administrative burden for the public. The target: A Lean organization that is oriented toward the individual. Lean is an improvement program that helps to achieve that target.

Lean: That's about Cars, Right?

The Lean improvement program originated in the Japanese automotive industry. More aptly put, Lean was concocted as a compilation of all sorts of smart methods and techniques, applied over many years and proved effective. This compilation is known as Lean Management because of its point of view—a lean and flexible organization. Not thin, not fat, just right.

Important basic principles of the Lean program include:

■ Putting the customer center stage
■ Adding value for the customer
■ Making wastes visible and eliminating them
■ Aiming for your employees to own the processes
■ Making your employees champions

Lean is very useful in the public sector if it aspires to these principles. Currently, a number of publications on the application of Lean in the office environment of the service industry are available. This book was specifically written from the perspective of the governmental organization because the environment and structure of a government organization is fundamentally different from that of a company. Companies have directors for management. Government organizations also are run by management, but in many cases they are accountable to the public as well. Every two or more years, the public elects the people to represent them in government offices.

A second important difference is the phenomenon of interest. Interest is very important for companies. Government organizations in most countries neither want to make a profit nor are they permitted to; however, sometimes a controller will issue an interest warning to a municipal government. This does not mean that interest is falling, but that there is a risk of interest originating. This is a signal to find ways to spend more money. Government organizations can run at a loss and even go technically bankrupt, but they cannot cease to exist.

A third remarkable difference with business is the notion of "the customer." For a company, it's very simple: customers wish to purchase the products or services. In the public sector, matters are more complicated. Individuals and companies are interested parties of the government, but they are not always the customer. Contrary to the business market, in government, individuals do not decide, purchase, or pay. The legislator decides, the citizen (individually or collectively) purchases and pays. Also, public servants do not negotiate the price of their services with individuals, or so we would hope. The citizen as a customer and other civil roles will be further discussed in Chapter 2.

Five Basic Principles in Lean

Lean in the profit sector has five basic principles (Womack and Jones, 1996) with a logical order:

1. *Add value*: Stop and ask yourself who the customer of the process is. Add value for your customer (explained in Chapter 2).
2. *Value stream mapping/learn to see wastes*: Map these processes and distinguish between value adding actions and wastes. Learn to detect these wastes and attack them (see Chapters 3 and 4).
3. *Create flow*: Direct the processes and the organization in such a way that flow is created. Are processes running smoothly without catches or quality issues (see Chapter 5)?
4. *Pull from the customer*: This fluid process has the same rate as the consumer's purchase behavior. It is not faster, because this creates inventory, but not any slower either, because then the customer has to wait, or may even decide not to purchase at all. Does it work the same in the public sector (see Chapter 5)?
5. *Aim for perfection*: Lean never stops. You will never attain the perfect situation, and, even if you do, environmental factors will change or your competitor will come up with something new, and as a result the situation will no longer be perfect (see Chapter 9).

The following chapters explain each principle, tailor-made for the public sector.

Chapter 2

Adding Value: Who Is the Customer?

Effective improvement management puts the customer center stage. An organization is doing the right thing when it adds value for the customer. Customers decide if an action, service, or product represent value to them. But who is the customer in the public sector, really? Is there such a thing as a customer?

In the business enterprise, the phenomenon of a customer is relatively easy to define. A customer is a person or business that purchases a commodity or service. The customer considers freely purchasing a product on the basis of the product's functionality, its look, image, and price. Companies put effort into making sure that the customer will buy the product, and will buy it from them. On the other hand, a company can choose not to deliver to a customer or use different prices for different customers. No delivery is made until there is a mutual agreement.

The phenomenon of the customer in the public sector is more complex. Public service providers are usually monopolists. The quality of service of, for example, the various municipalities is compared, but individuals and companies cannot choose between different suppliers of products.

Producers and service providers in the business sector offering unwanted products and services will eventually go bankrupt. Public organizations guide "customer demand" by making it mandatory through rules and regulations for the public to purchase particular services or products. This contributes substantially to a public organization's right to exist.

Companies usually aim to increase market share and attract more customers. This is not always the case with public institutions. Social

Services, for example, aim to lower their number of customers, and their direction of the cash flow (from supplier to "customer") is exactly opposite of that in a standard customer–supplier relationship.

Portrait of a Citizen

It's obvious to state at this point that public servants should regard individuals and businesses as customers. The question is whether that's always right. When you want to get somewhere and you choose public transportation, it's easy to imagine yourself as the customer and the public service provider as the supplier. You purchase the transport fare, but you have a choice—you could walk, ride a bike, drive. But, does the same hold true for the customer–supplier relationship where a tax assessment or permit is concerned?

Tax departments sometimes try to make their employees believe that the taxpayers are their customers, but the public's freedom of choice suggests otherwise. Insisting that the taxpayer is the customer seems a bit artificial. Citizens are not customers; they are required to pay taxes. It's not a matter of choice. This doesn't mean that the revenue service shouldn't be customer-friendly when dealing with the taxpayer. Some governmental organizations intuitively feel that the term *customer* doesn't apply, so they use the term *client* instead.

The term *citizen* should, for the scope of this chapter, be taken to indicate individual citizens, citizens in collective unions, and businesses. In this book, we distinguish between seven citizen roles:

The citizen as:

1. Customer
2. User
3. Subject
4. Voter
5. Taxpayer
6. Partner
7. Administrator

Customer

This is about the kind of governmental service agencies where citizens are customers, comparable to private service organizations. The citizen as

Figure 2.1

customer is a citizen with a choice of products or services and alternatives. The basis is one of voluntariness. A good example of a governmental service where the citizen is a customer is public transportation. Citizens can choose to take a bus, but there are alternatives, such as their own cars or bicycles (Figure 2.1).

Value in the eyes of the citizen as customer: The citizen assesses the quality of service in terms of punctuality, safety and convenience.

The role of the government: The government plays the part of service provider, largely comparable to that of a commercial business. The same principles hold for the commercial service provider. They want to be the fastest, cheapest, and the best, quality-wise. The government is growth-oriented toward the citizen–customer: the more, the merrier. So, it is hardly surprising that this type of service provision is privatized first. Some examples include:

- All forms of public transport
- Mail handling

User

Citizens use public facilities maintained by the government, such as roads, parks, libraries, and swimming-pools. The citizen, as a user, has a right to quality in his living environment; it has to be clean and safe and within reach.

Other types of facilities required by citizens include individual aids to guarantee participation in society for as long as possible. This type of facility is part of a request for assistance, such as the material needed to keep a person mobile (wheelchairs, walkers, and other aids), home care, or transportation for the disabled (Figure 2.2).

Figure 2.2

Value in the eyes of the citizen as user: Clean, transparent collective facilities immediately accessible to everybody, as well as individual facilities that are made to measure and immediately available to all.

The role of the government: Exploiting and maintaining the collective facilities. Quickly supplying citizens with the correct individual aids.

Examples of citizens as users of public facilities:

■ Visitors to swimming pools and parks
■ Local residents wanting to keep their area attractive and livable
■ Tourists

Examples of citizens as users of collective facilities:

■ An older person applying for a walker
■ Disabled students using special transportation to travel to school
■ Handling a report on a dangerous situation in the public space (like a pothole)

Subject

The citizen as a subject has a right to quality in order and authority. To guarantee order and authority, there have to be rules, which must be monitored. The government dictates, by means of legislation, rules and regulation. The government enforces these rules by issuing constraints—e.g., in the form of permits, but also by upholding the rules. The government decides that certain roads should have speed limits. They can enforce this by constructing roads in such a way that it becomes difficult to drive fast on these roads. They can install speed bumps or narrow or widen a road. In addition, the government regularly checks the speed of drivers, and violators are fined (Figure 2.3).

Value in the eyes of the citizen as subject: As a collective value, citizens want their government to treat all subjects equally regardless of their background,

Figure 2.3

and to do so explicitly. As an individual value, it should be noted for a citizen that a sanction is just, imposed fast, and without administrative cost.

The role of the government: The government makes transparent and unambiguous regulations and laws, and clearly maintains them. Examples include:

- Maintaining environmental laws by means of inspections by an environmental official
- Granting permits for home alterations
- Speed checks by traffic police

Voter

The citizen as a voter is a citizen who knows him- or herself to be represented and expects a certain quality of politics and administration. This is about the voting process itself and the way in which the voter can find his or her vote reflected by the political decision making.

Value for the citizen as a voter: The preparations for the elections and voting proceed in a clear and orderly fashion. Citizens can tell that the politicians show commitment and hold themselves accountable to the community (Figure 2.4).

The role of the government: Ensuring orderly elections; representing the voters. Examples include:

- Local council elections
- Referenda

Taxpayer

In order to perform its duties, the government levies taxes. The citizens as taxpayers may expect good use of their tax money. The government must work effectively and efficiently. Sometimes managers of tax departments can be heard saying that they regard citizens as customers. Citizens don't tend

Figure 2.4

Figure 2.5

to see it that way. It is true that citizens are offered a variety of services for their tax money, but they do not make the connection between the services rendered and the tax levied on them. If a sewer system is installed in your neighborhood, you may feel more like a public operations service customer than a tax department customer (Figure 2.5).

Value for the citizen as tax payer: The process of levying taxes is transparent, fast, and effective. The citizen feels that useful things are done with the money collected.

The role of the government: Collect money to maintain the smallest possible public organization and collective and individual services. Some examples include:

- Levying and collecting taxes to maintain and renovate the sewer system or collect garbage
- Premiums for medical expenses and disability

Partner

Citizens as partners want to collaborate with the government in the development of the town and in the livelihood of its citizens. This can be done in the economic field where forms of collaboration between business and government can lead to increased welfare, reduction of local unemployment, and improvement of living conditions in development areas. The government maintains these connections with organizations in civil society, such as voluntary organizations. These organizations are supported with public money; in return, they do something useful.

A special form of partnership is the collaboration between an unemployed person and the local social service office. When agreement is reached on the matter of benefit, there is mutuality (Figure 2.6). The unemployed person wants to be able to provide for himself. The government wants everybody to actively seek employment, or at least to be socially active. This helps create

Figure 2.6

a balance of rights and duties. Many departments of employment and social services, therefore, link the right to benefit from these services to the obligation of job search requirements.

Value for the citizen as a partner: Ideas of citizens (and businesses) are taken seriously and put into practice. An important value is the creation of ownership for citizens. Citizens do not really feel joint owners of their neighborhood until they are not only represented by politicians, but also are joint decision makers in matters concerning livability and safety. In addition, citizens can profit from a social safety net in the form of benefits in case of unemployment. For the citizens as a collective, there is a valuable incentive for the unemployed to find work and to end their benefit as soon as possible.

The role of the government: The government is responsible for developing a neighborhood area and also in assisting the citizens living there with their personal development. Examples include:

- Getting citizens involved in the development of a particular city area.
- Getting businesses involved in the development of a town's economy.
- Collaborating with charity organizations, which is the social and cultural duty of the government.
- Temporarily supplying citizens with money to provide for themselves, and assisting them in the process of finding suitable jobs.

Citizens Decide

The government is not usually an equal partner, but there are situations in which citizens can seriously advance their own interests. In Europe, we see a lot of experimentation with citizen participation in the development of neighborhoods. Citizens can decide what happens with an area.

Citizens are very interested in this, as it turns out. Mostly this amounts to citizens having a say in already far-advanced plans or stating their preference in a nonbinding referendum with a choice of three options. However, there are examples of citizens submitting their own plans. The local government first decides the conditions that these plans must meet, but the citizens, often united in interest groups, come up with the ideas. It is the government's duty to ensure that these interest groups are heard and to strive for consensus in an orderly fashion. Politicians have to be prepared for some pretty remarkable suggestions from citizens.

And then it is all about putting your money where your mouth is. Will the politicians keep their word and let the public decide? Will it really happen, or will the politicians cancel the entire idea and continue the process behind closed doors? There is a chance that some of the council members don't like the public's choices but don't want to offend them. That's when they start attacking the procedure, e.g., by saying that the result is not representative. People feel rejected and their faith in politicians is damaged.

Still, ownership of the neighborhood or area is an important value for citizens. When the citizens' choice is respected in the end and the government organizes the particular area according to the public's needs, it becomes apparent that residents, and neighboring citizens, feel responsible for their choice and show this by actively cooperating in maintaining quality in the area, by organizing crime watches or cleaning up litter.

Members of the public are always brimming with great initiative. If you are a public service provider, don't stay in your office all the time or else you won't be aware of this initiative.

A fine example of successful citizen participation comes from the Lichtenberg district of Berlin, Germany. After years of deficits, the district's government decided to clarify all revenues and expenditure to the residents. At the same time, it was decided that the public should have decision-making power over a large part of the budget, the so-called Citizen Budget. At the beginning of each cycle, the public has several weeks to hand in proposals. Next, meetings are held, and opinions are voiced. The public can vent their thoughts on the proposals via a Web site as well. Afterwards, a group of citizens and a selected editorial team pick a number of proposals and put them up for vote. Following this, votes are cast online and via the mail, and a budget is drawn up. On the Lichtenberg Web site, anyone interested can read the proposals. District residents have seen their money going where they requested through their vote, which is toward cycling paths, modernizing the library, cultural and sports facilities, or youth club activities. Here is a strong example of the Lean thinking principle: putting the citizen first.

Administrator

Citizens who want to be politically active can become council members or chairmen in a municipal government, or senators, or members of a chamber.

Figure 2.7

Citizen administrators can influence how a neighborhood, town, or country is governed (Figure 2.7). They are not public servants, but a type of internal "customer" of the public servant's body.

Value for citizens as administrators: Administrators want to be informed clearly and comprehensively on all business relevant to the administration of a city. In actual practice, over-processing is one of the major pitfalls in the relationship between public servant and administrators. The civil service turns out huge reports, hefty annual estimates, and a tsunami of indicators that make it very difficult to distinguish the outlines. Administrators sometimes wonder if it is really impossible to fit some reports onto a single sheet of paper. Conversely, the principle holds that anything you report may be held up for questioning or requests for further clarification.

The role of the government (as a public servant): Reporting clearly, concisely, and quickly on all information and advice relevant to administrators. Some examples include:

- Processes of the planning and control cycle, such as the realization of the estimate and annual account
- Process of the realization of a policy document

Critical Quality Parameters

The fact that public organizations distinguish between these seven citizen roles shows that contact between public servant and citizen can take several forms. Sometimes the relationship is equal, sometimes it is not. A public servant nearly always has to deal with several interested parties. Often it concerns the interests of the individual citizen and public interests. These interests can sometimes conflict, which can result in some pretty odd situations. For instance, often citizens think that the government should play the part of the strict enforcer of rules and laws, and at the same time feel that the police officer fining them for a traffic violation should show more understanding for their situation and not be so petty about things.

Actually, citizens are always interested parties to any government organization, whether active (by applying for a permit or passport) or passive. In most governmental services, three parties are involved: the two parties of the transaction, namely the public servant and the citizen that has requested the service, and as a third party, society itself—the neighbors and taxpayers. The role of the citizen as a customer is the only capacity in which there is no direct third interested party.

So, is it useful to distinguish between these various citizen roles? It is fine to call citizens customers or clients when dealing with them. Someone applying for welfare at the social services would certainly be surprised when addressed with "partner." But, for the redesigning of processes it can create problems.

If we consider citizens customers all of the time, processes could become very Lean indeed. To someone applying for a building permit, the statutory publication duty and time frame set for citizens to file an objection is not value-adding, but a waste. It's waiting time, after all. If the process of granting permits were Lean, and the applicant played the role of a customer, all waiting time would be eliminated because where the applicant is concerned the process at this point is a stalemate and no value is being added.

The ideal process for a citizen or a business applying for a permit is to apply for the permit by telephone or Internet, and then get it at once—or even better, no permit at all, because we can go on very well without that piece of paper. However, citizens in a collective, such as the applicant's neighbors, feel that waiting time definitely adds value. It gives them the opportunity to file an objection to the application for a building permit.

Although these different citizen roles can complicate a service official's approach to the citizen or business in question, some critical quality parameters remain unaltered, regardless of the citizen's role. These quality parameters are:

- Speed
- Punctuality
- Correctness
- Clarity (e.g., readability)

Those against include:

- The lowest costs
- And, for citizens and businesses, a minimum of or no administrative costs

This means that when improving processes it can still be decided if something adds value or not, from the point of view of the individual citizen, and that the same must be considered from the point of view of a citizen collective. Citizens in the role of taxpayers may not be happy with their tax assessment, but they expect absolute transparency, for things to add up, and for the transaction not to drag on. In addition, the taxpayer feels that if his situation is much like that of the guy next door, he should be paying at least the same amount of tax.

Chapter 3

Determine Value

A process is a sequence of actions in a deliberate and logical order, or so we should hope, with a specified result in mind. This result is either an object or a service. Processes consist of actions that either create value or waste as far as the public is concerned. Whether it's the production of peanut butter or a service rendered to a member of the public, employees must be able to rely on processes to carry out their tasks and create value for the "customer." One advantage of industrial production processes is that wastes are clearly visible. Everyone can see that a production machine has stopped or that there's too much inventory in store. From administrative processes, the status is hardly visible; we are left wondering if there's still continuity in the process or if everything has stopped, and how much of the "product" is still under way? Much of the process takes place inside people's heads or with computers. As a result, it's difficult to follow or measure the progress of an administrative process. However, it's not impossible. To do this, two categories of process activities must be distinguished: (1) those that create value and (2) those that do not. Take the following situation:

> You are driving along the freeway. Your fuel gauge tells you it's time to get gas. You leave the freeway via the exit ramp to the filling station, where you park your car next to a gasoline pump. You switch off the engine, unbuckle your seatbelt, open the door, get out of the car, and close the door. You walk around the car to open the gas valve and screw off the top. You stick the nozzle in the gas tank and allow the fluid to flow into it. When your tank is

full, the pump switches off, and you can now replace the nozzle. Next, you close the valve and go inside to pay. Afterward, you get back into your car and drive off.

This is a process with a number of actions. The specific aim is put fuel in the tank. The entire process takes approximately six minutes. As far as the driver-customer is concerned, there's only one moment in this process when value is created, and that's when the fuel flows into the tank. This takes about one minute. All other actions are forms of waste; in this process, they take up 83% of the time. Most of these actions appear to be inevitable wastes because to get the fuel in your tank, you will have to get out of your car and unscrew the valve cap of your gas tank. And paying and getting back in the car seem pretty inevitable, too. Still, it's good to consider these actions as wastes because this invites a good hard look to see if they can be eliminated. Still, for a customer in a hurry, the ideal situation is a fuel process without all of this inevitable waste—as in just getting the gas into the tank, preferably while driving, just like air force aircraft that gets fueled up while airborne. This way of looking helps us to go back to what is really essential: to create value for the customer and eliminate all waste. This is how original and radical process improvements are born—for example, tank robots that open the valve, unscrew the cap, and screw it back on again, and presto, fewer actions to go. Scientists are looking into the possibility of cars getting fueled up with energy from the road surface.

It remains essential to reason from the customer's point of view. When I go for gas, I may be in a hurry. Still, I sometimes see people sitting over a cup of coffee, talking. It looks as if these folks place a lot of value on the social activity, while getting gas is little more than a side issue to them.

The Eight Deadly Wastes

Whether an action creates value is determined by what point of view the member of the public takes in one of his seven citizen roles. Does the citizen see the value of an action? Having a document signed by an executive may be very useful as far as an organization is concerned, but the citizen does not see the value of it. Any action without value in the eyes of the citizen is called *waste*. There are eight different types of waste.

1. Defects
2. Rework and correction
3. Inspection
4. Waiting
5. Inventory
6. Transport
7. Overprocessing
8. Insufficient used of talent and creativity

The eight deadly wastes are explained below:

Defects

Ideal processes turn out products or services that are right the first time. Process or handling errors may result in products or services that do not meet the client's expectations or the legal standards. Flawed products or services may sometimes be adapted or repaired. Defects always lead to extra effort and cost, and they don't create value in the eyes of the customer (Figure 3.1). On the contrary, they cause irritation. Some examples include:

■ Sending documents to the wrong addresses
■ Wrong data input
■ Unjustified awards/rejections

Rework and Correction

Reworking is repeatedly working on a product or the repeated performance of a service. More time and material are spent on a service that failed to meet the standard before. A major part of the work of call centers that

Defects

Figure 3.1

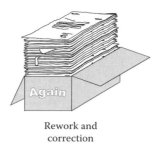

Rework and
correction

Figure 3.2

form the front office of many public organizations is a form of reworking. Documents sent to customers' homes are unclear or downright confusing. So, customers call the call center, where someone proceeds to give them the same information again.

Another annoying example of reworking is asking for what is already known, as, for instance, in the case of asking a member of the public the same information at each counter and recording it every time in yet another system. Persons well known at one service are considered new at the next and, subsequently, subjected to yet another round of the same questions (Figure 3.2). The ideal situation is using a single creator of information with multiple users. Examples include:

■ Resending documents
■ Drawing up policy documents more than once
■ Dealing with justified complaints

Inspection

There is a relationship between the measure of control and the reliability of processes. The less reliable a process, the more control is exerted on the operation of the process and the more numerous the checks on the products resulting from this process. If we take this argument to its logical conclusion, it means that a waterproof process does not require checks (Figure 3.3).

Checks can be obligatory or temporarily necessary, but they do not create value as far as the customer is concerned. Organizations that spend a lot of time and money on checks and have several staff services dedicated to this exude an atmosphere of reliability, while, in fact, these organizations suggest that they do not sufficiently trust their processes or their employees.

Inspection

Figure 3.3

There's a Dutch saying, which in translation goes something like this: "A butcher never does his own meat inspection." While this is, in fact, not true—there must be numerous butchers who inspect their own meats—what is truly remarkable about the saying is that it reflects a cherished notion, not just felt by the Dutch, that people cannot be trusted with the inspection of their own products and services, and that they should always be checked on by another person, preferably an outside party. Actually, people are quite capable of being their own judge. Likewise, employees are often perfectly capable of deciding independently if something meets or fails the quality standards.

The government's actions are fueled by some kind of fear, based on potential consequences of decisions. Are unwanted precedents being created? Often, a public servant carrying out a job doesn't take responsibility for a decision, but takes it up with a superior. It is difficult for a public servant to say yes. Someone is always asked to cover them. What's more, if, after an endless red-tape labyrinth, a document sporting four persons' initials falls on your desk, would you, as the last person in line, not sign it, too? Examples include:

- A sign-till-you-drop culture (the boss has to okay everything)
- Check and *double check*; checking the same quality aspect several times
- Checking for improper use where improper use is ruled out

Waiting

Processes only create value if they result in products and services that meet customer requirements. If an administrative process comes to a standstill because the required documents are piled on some employee's desk awaiting further processing or a signature, no value is being created for the present. This form of waste is often clearly visible in the form of piles on desks or overflowing digital in-boxes. When the process covers several desks or departments, or when it's part of a chain process, the sum of all the piles

Waiting

Figure 3.4

in the in-trays and out-trays can be gargantuan. And, the final result is that people are kept waiting (Figure 3.4). Some examples include:

- Waiting for information from other departments or chain partners
- Waiting for colleagues who work part-time or are absent for other reasons
- Waiting for information from the applicant

Inventory

In administrative processes, "inventory" is the sum of all tasks waiting to be processed (e.g., the total number of applications or complaints that need attention). Inventory may be a result of the administration department routinely processing in batches; processing is halted because people wait for a stack of applications to first pile up. Alternatively, they stick to routines, such as: "Tuesday is application-processing day." This may be efficient for the department, but not as far as the applicant is concerned.

Physical inventory is the sometimes excessive amount of office equipment and brochures, bought and paid for but seldom, if ever, used (Figure 3.5). Inventory is buying or creating something without capitalizing on it. A frequent variation on the theme is the amount of policy in inventory, for which there is no executive capacity.

Inventory

Figure 3.5

Figure 3.6 A fly-over near Brecht (Belgium) that was constructed in the 1980s but will never be connected to any highway, ever.

Another exceptional example of inventory is what is known as "lost highways." Sometimes the government has plans to construct a road. A final decision has yet to be reached, but the construction of a fly-over as part of the highway has already been commissioned. Sometimes the plans for a highway are abandoned after the fly-over has been constructed. Figure 3.6 shows a fly-over near Brecht (Belgium) that was constructed in the 1980s. It is not going to be connected to any highway, ever.

Examples of excess inventory include:

■ Inventory of applications for public services filed but not dealt with yet
■ Policies made and agreed upon, waiting to be implemented
■ Inventory of never-been-used office equipment
■ Building constructions that are never used

Transport

The route of paper or digital information in any organization can be long. Documents, analog or digital, can take weeks to get where they are going, or even get lost in a maze of red tape (Figure 3.7). This waste is expressed even more strongly over the complete chain because the transport of data and documents over all chain partners covers many desks.

Transport

Figure 3.7

Also, after transport, a document often faces a wait time; the recipient does not get cracking right away, but leaves the document to simmer and mature in the in-tray.

In addition, the government tends to use the public as data couriers by requiring that they bring along all sorts of documents that have been issued by yet other governmental agencies. Said information is digitally available but is printed out and handed to the member of the public in question, who proceeds to hand over said document to yet another official at yet another counter, where the printed information is digitized once more. Examples of this include:

- Data transport: The route an application makes past all sorts of officials down the chain
- The client moves: The route the client makes through the administrative maze of all sorts of counters
- Moving to the tune of "I will put you through to my colleague …"

Overprocessing

A minimum of time is needed to turn out a quality product or service. When more time (work) is spent on a product or service than is strictly necessary, we call it *overprocessing*. A well-known form of overprocessing is the production of a thick glossy report when a convenient single sheet of paper would have sufficed (Figure 3.8). But, well, you see, how can a memorandum of just one page be any good?

Another form of overprocessing is making a product, introducing rules, or offering a service for which no one is waiting. Rules and regulations are

Overprocessing

Figure 3.8

necessary. They offer security to the public, help protect the environment and ecology, ensure fair competition, and aim to make everybody as much a part of society as possible. However, rules and regulations can be superfluous when they serve no purpose in society, or even form a hindrance. A famous example is the European rule, abolished in 2010, that imposed all sorts of constraints on the crookedness of cucumbers.

A special variation on overprocessing comes from the municipal district heating of the city of Moscow. During the severe Russian winters, this district heating works so well that the average temperature of the connected homes is around 77° F. This is a good reason for many Muscovites to buy air conditioners to cool their homes during the brutal winters.

Examples of overprocessing include:

■ Jazzed up and unnecessarily fattened reports and policy documents
■ Sending e-mails and ccing the entire organization
■ Reclaiming $1.62 from a member of the public
■ Sending information to the public that will be thrown away unread
■ Cultural grants for shows playing to empty venues

Insufficient Use of Talent and Creativity

Every public body has employees in its service with some measure of talent to do their job even better and smarter, and to serve the public better to boot. Processes are often based on the principles of integrity, equality, and controllability. If unsolicited advice and creative improvement ideas go unappreciated by their managers, public servants tend to develop into individuals who just do their job on automatic pilot (Figure 3.9). But, because they need an outlet for their talent and creativity, they throw themselves head over heels into hobbies and charities. As a public servant once put it: "That's where I feel human."

The same holds for the general public. Our society is full of people with talents in all sorts of areas—e.g., the talent to take care of people, even as

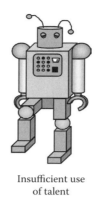

Insufficient use
of talent

Figure 3.9

a volunteer, or the talent to conceive creative ideas that benefit society, the neighborhood, or town. Not to apply this talent is a form of waste as well.

Another form of insufficient use of talent is having highly qualified staff do simple administrative tasks. Some examples include:

■ Leaving the creative potential of one's own employees untapped
■ Leaving the creative potential of the public untapped
■ A lawyer checking accounts or doing secretarial jobs

Avoidable and Unavoidable Waste

Waste can't be eliminated at the drop of a hat. There is a distinction between avoidable and unavoidable waste. Control may have been built into the process in order to intercept defects and may be useful at the moment. To reduce the number of checkups or eliminate them altogether, the cause of the defect first must be eliminated. Once the process has become more reliable, checkups still can be reduced or eliminated. Checking in this example is avoidable waste. You should always regard checkups as something temporary, necessary only for the moment, to intercept or avoid defects or possible improper use. Everything that can be done, must be done to make a process error-free and the chance of improper use nonexistent, so that checkups can be reduced or discontinued. Sometimes, however, monitoring can be a legal obligation—an unavoidable waste. Still, it's wise not to call waste "unavoidable" too easily. Before you know it, you'll accept all wastes.

There is no waste in an ideal process. "No waste" means that a member of the public receives the right product or service, of the right quality, exactly when needed, for a price he or she is willing to pay, and without having to go out of the way for it. The ideal process is not called "ideal" for nothing; it has not been reached yet. However, through continuous improvement, the ideal waste-free process can be more closely achieved.

Process improvement in the public sector means that all wastes in these processes are eliminated. Removing waste has resulted in drastically reduced process lead times and impressive improvements in the quality of what these processes yield. The aim is to improve service provision, perfectly tuned to the member of the public's request, with a more efficient and cheaper organization as a result.

Action Time and Lead Time

Practical Example

A financial supervisor can fine a financial organization (such as a bank or insurance company) in case of a violation. The financial organization may file a written objection against this fine. The supervisor should notify an organization that filed a complaint of the receipt of the complaint, after which the complaint is taken into consideration—a slow and painstaking process.

Sending a letter of receipt doesn't look like a gigantic obstacle at first glance. The complaint, however, makes a journey from the mailroom via secretarial offices to the person who will convert it into a confirmation of receipt and then send it back again. It's a route awash with opening, noting, recording, relocating, and signing. In all, it takes employees a total of 171 minutes just to handle the confirmation of receipt. That's 171 minutes action time. The process lead time starts the moment the complaint drops onto the supervisor's doormat, so to speak, and continues until the confirmation of receipt is in the mailbox of the financial organization. The lead time in this example is on average 15 days. In sum, that's 171 minutes of action time and 15 days on the road.

A process is a concatenation of actions that result in a product or service. If you travel alongside the product or service that results from this process,

Table 3.1 Different Kinds of Time in Processes

What Kind of Time	*Description*
Action time	The time that an action takes
Value-creating time	The time that a value-creating action takes
Lead time	The time between the beginning of a process until the end of the process; or, alternatively, the sum of all action times and wait times of a process

it's a journey full of surprises; one of deadlock, transformation, and transposition. Of the eight deadly wastes, "waiting" is a huge player in the process described above.

It isn't necessary for the 171 minutes of action time to be completely value creating. Opening an envelope, putting a document in a tray, filling out a register—in the eyes of a member of the public, none of this creates value. It is just transposition: a form of deadly waste. The only value-creating minutes are the 38 spent on reading the appeal thoroughly and drawing up a standard letter to acknowledge receipt, the transformation part. The rest is sheer waste. Read more about this example process in Chapter 4.

Chances are that with administrative processes the majority of time spent is time spent on waste. The total value-creating time (the time that something valuable happens as far as a member of the public is concerned (e.g., to an application) is just a fraction of the total lead time and only a part of the total action time (Table 3.1).

The number of transfer moments is indicative for process lead times. There are municipalities that use an operating process for granting food and liquor licenses that require a sturdy 35 transfer moments, plus an impressive 9 signatures. Each transfer moment is good for a minimum of one extra day of transfer time.

Action Time for the Citizen

In this time of consumer convenience, companies can still decide to have their customers execute a part of the process or production process. You can buy closets ready-made, but you also can buy them as a package. This is action time, too, only this time it's the customer's action time. The burden of assembling or not understanding the instructions or discovering that parts are missing is for the customer, who will put up with it (or some of it) because he paid less for it.

In the public sector, the member of the public is put to work as well. The administrative burden for members of the public consists of the costs (in time and money) spent by them so as to comply with government instructions on supplying information. Examples of this include: having to transport oneself to an official counter, sitting in a waiting room of a government building, talking with public servants, and filling out documents or having them filled out. There are two kinds of administrative burdens:

1. Administrative burden when exercising one's rights:
   a. Access to government information (request permission to inspect records)
   b. Participation in government plans (participation in zoning plans)
   c. Complaint and appeal procedures (appealing a tax assessment)
   d. Claim to means (application for a grant or a wheelchair)
2. Administrative burden as a result of complying with governmentally enforced obligations:
   a. Completing an application form for a permit (environmental permit, building permit)
   b. Notifications (change of address, birth)
   c. Supplying documents (for tax assessment or importing goods)
   d. Performing a medical checkup (for the right to medical facilities)

The average adult citizen spends between five and ten hours every year on officially enforced administrative matters. This includes such matters as applying for a passport or driver's license, completing tax papers, or applying for permits. That's an average.

Studies have shown that a mainstream healthy citizen in employment has the lightest administrative burden. Enterprising citizens and weaker members of society are the most heavily burdened, relatively speaking. Enterprising citizens feel restricted by an overload of laws and regulations by the government, which seems to want to thwart their plans more than to stimulate them. And if there's any governmental incentive, such as a subsidy, it comes at a price: a stack of forms to be filled out for application and assessment. As an entrepreneur once quipped, "… a public servant is nothing but a government-appointed 'curber'."

The weak in society, the elderly, the unemployed, the chronically ill, and the disabled experience an above-average administrative burden. These are individuals who, for physical or financial reasons, frequently have to deal with governmental agencies, and who often have to make great efforts to meet the administrative requirements. Front-runner in the race for the highest administrative burden would be a chronically ill single mother with a disabled, school-age child, living in subsidized housing, part-time unemployed, because she's looking for a part-time job and has plans to get married.

The way in which these highly burdened groups regard the government speaks volumes. The enterprising group thinks the government should not interfere with their business. The not-so-strong part of society thinks the government should be more helpful.

Creating Value in the Public Sector

To decide if a process action is value-creating or wasteful, look at it with the eyes of the customer. In commercial organizations, this is simple. Customers are those who buy our products. In any profit organization, an action creates value if:

- ■ The action is first-time right
- ■ A transformation takes place (not a translocation, but a desired change)
- ■ The customer wants to pay for it

The first two attributes of value creation are manageable in the public sector. Concerning the third, the member of the public is not always the customer of public processes, but can also play another role. The member of the public as a consumer of services doesn't always have to pay for the services. Some services or permits are free to the user—i.e., paid for with tax money. Sometimes members of the public receive money, as in cases of benefit or subsidy. The third attribute of creating value should be adapted to suit the proposition that a particular action must be useful in the eyes of the citizens as individuals and in the eyes of the citizens as a collective. It must also be useful enough for people to want to pay a tax for it. Again:

- ■ The action is first-time right
- ■ A transformation takes place (not a translocation, but a desired change)
- ■ The individual wants to pay taxes for it

In Chapter 2, we made a distinction between the various citizen roles. In this paragraph, we will look at a number of examples of process analysis, focusing on the question: What constitutes value?

Subsidy

Groups of citizens dedicate themselves to culture, sports, and social events. This could be a voluntary organization or a commercial one, such as a theater company, which can be subsidized by the government. Sometimes the government and the organization agree on required results, but in many cases the government grant should be considered a token of appreciation and encouragement. These organizations are not government customers. You might argue that they are suppliers; the process of awarding grants is quite similar to a purchasing process. Citizens requesting a grant do so in the role of user of a governmental service provision—in this case, money. For the citizen, the value is added at the moment the money is transferred. All other administrative actions in the grant process by government and members of the public are wastes in the eyes of the applicant.

Grants are tax money. Members of the public who pay taxes want the government to use that money wisely, which means that no tax money should be wasted on, for instance, theatrical productions playing to empty venues. Therefore, for this collective of citizens, value is created if subsidies are only granted to useful institutions that spend their money wisely, and demonstrably so. For the applicant, this is nothing more than inspection—one of the eight deadly wastes.

Is Answering Questions Value Adding?

A federal government agency provides special permits for individuals who are on the payroll of a transportation company and want to drive a truck. Most drivers make a phone call to the agency to apply for that permit. An employee of a call center answers the phone and sends an application form by mail. The truck driver fills out the form and sends it back along with references of good character, a copy of his drivers license, a recent photo, and some papers from his employer. So far so good. Let's see what happens. The first phone call, the driver requests the license. The second phone call, he asks for information about how to fill out the extensive application form. Three other phone calls, the call-center employee answers the truck driver's questions ("How about my permit?") politely and with a smile ("It's on the way, sir").

Is the call center adding value?

The first call seems necessary because otherwise the agency would not know he wants a permit. The second call is polite and helpful, but not necessary. This phone call is redundant if the application form and the written explanation are clearly written. Because of the long leadtime (six weeks) of this process, the average truck driver calls three times after sending his application for just one permit.

From the truck driver's point of view, only the first phone call is adding value. The other four are sheer waste. He is eager to drive a truck and the delays are frustrating. The call center is busy all day answering questions, trying to help people. But the center is adding value only 20 percent of the time.

The Extension

A cramped homeowner on a quiet street wants to add an extension to his house to create more space. This requires a considerable transposition of the rear of the house, plus the existing extension on top of the garage annexed to the house. The government has decreed that for such home improvements a permit is required. This regulation was conceived to protect the neighbors of the family against possible downsides, to the building plans.

One downside could be that the neighbor's extension could block out their daylight. For this reason, publication requirements are stipulated in the building permission process. Each application for a building permit is published by the council. From the day of publication, for a period of three weeks, any citizen has the right to object to the intended construction. The applicant must wait. The applicant for the permit is not a customer, but a subject. Waiting is one of the deadly wastes for the applicant, but, in our example, not for the neighbors. You might even suggest that the next-door neighbors are "customers" here. Three weeks wait time is valuable as far as the neighbors are concerned.

The Traffic Violation

If a driver speeds, he or she may expect a speeding ticket in the mailbox three months after the violation is observed with a speed camera. The ticket tells you where, when, and at what time violation of the speed limit took place. It is hard to maintain that the process of transforming an established offense into a ticket is one in which the offender is a customer. The government has limited the maximum speed on the road in question and checks to see if the public abides by it. The speed limit was created to ensure the safety of residents and other road users, and for reasons of livability. With a little imagination, you could say that the residents and other road users in this scenario are interested parties in their citizen role as users. They want to be able to live safely and pleasantly in the vicinity of this road, and feel safe on it. To them it is important that the government takes action when this rule is violated. The offender is a subject. Value for the residents is embedded in the moment that the offender sets eyes on his speeding ticket, as a means to improve road safety. It would be oversimplifying if one were to say that the entire process in the eyes of the offender as a subject is waste. From the point of view of the offender, there is much room for improvement in this process. A three-month wait for the fine to arrive is way too long. The citizen in question has to dig deep for the facts: Where was I going that day? Why was I speeding? Was it me, or was it my partner? In the ideal process, the offender receives his speeding ticket when he comes home or checks his e-mail, on the day of his offense. And when will the neighborhood notice a drop in speeding?

The Street Party

In some cities, working-class neighborhoods tend to be characterized by a strong sense of community. On hot summer days, this is often expressed by impromptu plans for a street barbecue on the weekend. So, the residents want to block off the street, deck it out, and put lots of tables and chairs out. The government has put a stop to this; every street party requires a permit, and, the application time for this permit is four weeks. The residents are not customers for this permit, but are cast in the role of the government's subjects. Thus, the spontaneous idea has been nipped in the bud. The street party permit was conceived to prevent parts of the town from becoming inaccessible for emergency services, such as the fire department and the ambulance. In addition, the fire department likes to know where the bigger BBQs are held. So, you could argue that society and the emergency services are the interested parties for this permit. The four-week wait doesn't create value because no publication is required and the wait time is due only to the public servant not handling the request at once. In practice, the city has never turned down an application for a street party. So, for this process to be ideal there would be no permit procedure, but a simple announcement of a street party. The citizen reports the planned street party to the council no later than one day before the set date so the fire brigade and the ambulance service can be informed. As a reward, the citizen receives a decoration package for decking out the street.

Rightfulness and Efficiency

Citizens can play two roles at once. Sometimes the citizen is part of a larger group whose interests are protected and defended by the government. However, as an individual, the citizen's interests may seriously conflict with the public interest. In these cases, there is a conflict of roles. Weighing individual versus public interest is an important function of the government. A citizen who thinks that the government is not firm enough and acts randomly, and who blames the decline in quality of his living environment on the government's attitude, also may consider the government too strict and rigid when he finds his own interest thwarted when a request for a permit is turned down.

Processes in the public sector are usually drawn from policies, legislation, and with the ease and convenience of the internal organization in mind. The quality of a process is tested by considering its rightfulness (Is this fair?), efficiency (Is this a good way to go about it?), and effectiveness (Are we serving both the public's and the individual's case?) The first—rightfulness—is emphasized strongly in the design of official processes. The government wants to avoid any appearance of unfairness. The government cannot and will not negotiate prices, has to treat every individual in the same circumstances equally, and must abide by laws and regulations. If the government won't do it, who will? Efficiency and effectiveness take a back seat. What is often the case is that something passes the test of rightfulness and the rest does not weigh so heavily. If the statutory maximum term for issuing a permit is eight weeks, people will do anything to realize this within the eight weeks, but no more than that.

The strong focus on rightfulness results in extremely complex processes with many checkups. Public servants check members of the public and each other. Still, to some extent, all this checking only provides a semblance of security. Citizens are asked to fill out all sorts of statements before the government provides a service. (As if any of these people filling in statements are likely to notify the government of their intentions to be fraudulent.) In reality, these forms look as if they have been conceived to structure the work of the employees more so than to prevent improper use. And what's more, is every member of the public really a potential crook? Of course not. In the social service and tax processes that have been made Lean, you can see that people work with risk profiles. Only citizens that fit certain criteria are watched. That helps to avoid a lot of work because the majority of the public does not need to be checked or checked so frequently.

Checks are one of the eight deadly wastes. Checks can be necessary, but they do not create value. To consider checks a form of waste is an incentive to constantly look for ways to reduce their number or even remove them altogether. Examples can include the following:

The Constant Handicap

School-going disabled residents of a city have a right to free transportation to school. To avail oneself of this, a doctor's certificate is required. This free student transport ticket needs to be extended annually, and an annual visit to the doctor must be paid to get the certificate. This takes a citizen on average four hours. A little girl fails to understand why she has to go and see a doctor every year to explain why the legs she lost in a tragic accident haven't grown back.

Mobile Citizens

A large municipality doesn't want to see its residents tied to their homes and so puts a lot of stock and store by their mobility. For residents who have difficulty walking, some facilities are available, such as a rollator (a walking frame on wheels). A doctor decides if the citizen has the right to this free service. Because of lack of staff and red tape, the application takes on average 13 weeks to accomplish. The public servants did the math and discovered that the costs of the number of hours spent by the municipality on the application and the doctor's certificate must be 20 times as much as the purchase price of the rollator ($100). Sometimes, because of the long lead time, the applicant had died before the rollator was delivered. Therefore, some time ago the idea was conceived that, to accommodate the applicant, the rollator would be delivered awaiting approval. That's one step ahead. But, a simple study shows that requests for rollators are practically never turned down. So, what would happen if we just simply handed over a rollator the very same day if someone asks for one? Would the entire city suddenly start walking with rollators? The chances of improper use are quite small. Applicants have some personal obstacles to overcome before they apply for one of these things. These insights have shortened the process from 13 weeks to two days and doctor's certificates are no longer required. But, what if people start applying for a scooter? They're fun, and they go a lot faster, too.

Money for a Bicycle

A social service agency stimulates people who are receiving compensation pay and who want retraining to get a job. The incentive consists of paying for the training and paying for a bus ticket or a bicycle to help them get to the school. Public servants who are blinded by the rule of rightfulness want to prevent giving money for a bicycle to those who already own one. So, that is why unannounced house calls are made. There's a case of a member of the public who was visited seven times, but was never home. The eighth time, she was in, and there was a bicycle in the shed. "That's my son's," the woman said. "We are not giving you money for a bicycle," the public servant replied. The woman lodged a complaint, but it was rejected. She appealed. She won her case, and the $350 to buy a bicycle. By then, some $10,000 in time had been spent on the incident.

The team was put to the test on how to improve this process. The question was raised: What will happen if we stop checking? Some people will make improper use of the facility. Is that bad? Well, it's $350 each time. Why did we come up with the bicycle regulation in the first place? As an incentive for the unemployed who decided to put energy into training, with a focus on getting a job. The team decided to not perform checks any longer.

Are All Members of the Public Potential Crooks?

Employees from governmental organizations who are schooled in the principles of Lean Management, and who want to eliminate deadly waste, are constantly considering the reason behind a particular checkup and the consequences of it, only to remove the checkup from the process after a solid risk analysis and replace it by random checks later on, or to stop pouring energy into it. Once an organization has started with Lean, the discussion quickly moves to the topic of how far the public may be trusted. Hardliners among the public servants want to hold on to checkups. In their opinion of humankind, all members of the public are untrustworthy until proof of the contrary, which is done by means of checks and random checks—and all of this while they are citizens themselves. A method more in line with Lean is: The public is trustworthy until proof to the contrary.

Insurance companies wrestle with the same principle. If someone files a claim, do you mistrust this and check it out? Or do you trust the policyholder and do you agree and award compensation? One large insurance company wanted to start working according to this latter principle and did the following to make their employees experience a change in perception. They removed all cashiers from the company restaurant where all employees ate lunch. Employees got their own lunch, paid for it at the unmanned register, and got their change themselves. Random checks are run at low frequency. It's operating on trust. The company management's motto is: "If we can't even trust our own people, we definitely can't trust our customers."

Chapter 4

Mapping the Value Stream

Administrative processes are largely invisible. Everything takes place in the heads of the process players. Processes appear, fragmentarily, as stacks of paper on desks, or in computers. You can't improve invisible processes.

An important tool to make processes visible is a value stream map (VSM). A VSM is not a standard process description, but rather enables you to track the route of a product or service through an organization. To put it graphically, you pretend to be an application for a government service and record through the VSM everything that happens to you along the way: what treatment you get, where you're put down, how long you lie there, and at what junction you will be changed from the application into the service—the requested transformation.

VSMs are little more than practical tools to get the discussion going on how to create value for the individual and detect waste inside processes. It starts off with asking who the interested parties to a process are. They can be individual citizens, a collective of citizens, or an internal customer, such as the council or other public servants. Three types of processes may be distinguished here (Figure 4.1):

1. Primary processes
2. Governing processes
3. Auxiliary processes

The clients of primary processes are citizens in one or more of their citizen roles, and the processes concerned include granting licenses, levying tax, or dealing with complaints. These processes are mostly executive.

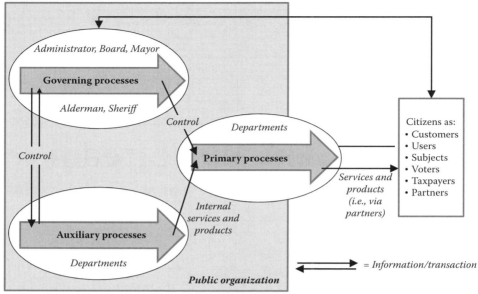

C. Paardekooper, B. Teeuwen 2008

a

b

Figure 4.1

Table 4.1 Three Kinds of Processes

Kind of Process	Primary	Governing	Auxiliary
Interested parties	Citizens (in six citizen roles)	Management, councils, secretaries, and staff	Public servants, departments, management, and councils
Examples	Granting permits Writing tickets Subsidy processes	Planning and control processes Policy processes	Mail processing Salary processing

The governing processes are the ones that the government organization uses to manage its area of responsibility. These may be policy processes, but may also be planning and control processes. Internal public servants and the council are the clients of these processes.

The third group is that of the auxiliary processes. These processes touch on every level of the organization, from mail processing and settling invoices to paying salaries.

All three kinds of processes can be mapped well with the use of VSM (Table 4.1). The public usually notices the improvement in primary processes quite clearly, because these improve the quality of service.

However, before we sketch the current process using a VSM, we must consider to what extent the process has a right to exist at all. We do so by answering the following questions:

1. *Who are the interested parties and what role does the citizen take?*
   It is important to decide in the process where and for whom value is created and what the wastes are.
2. *Why was this process and this service conceived?*
   It sounds strange, but employers of governmental organizations sometimes have to think hard about why a particular process is there at all. Sometimes they only manage to cite the statutory provisions, while, in fact, a societal effect was the aim.
3. *Are the process and the service necessary? What will happen if we stop it altogether?*
   It is possible that the societal effect that was the aim is not being attained, or is being attained by another policy with a corresponding process. Would the public notice if we stopped it altogether? Is interference from the government really necessary?

4. *Can we combine the process with another, similar process?*
   For instance, what if we merged all license processes relating to building and renovating into a single process with a single set of questions?
   A question of a different order is: Should we do this ourselves? Or
   should we outsource the execution of the process (e.g., to an organization that has experience doing this for similar governmental organizations)? This has been happening for some time in Shared Service
   Centers or with private or semiprivate companies, with the government
   in the role of principal or director.
5. *Can we think of other approaches with the same result?*
   For example, should we ask for a notification only, instead of demanding a permit?

Mapping the Current State

With the answers to these questions as a starting point, it's possible to map
the current value stream. Improving processes starts with knowing the current situation. By sketching the current situation, people learn to distinguish
waste. Only if the answer to question 3 above is a well-founded "we might
as well stop" can a process description be eliminated.

A clear idea, supported by facts, of the customer's request, the process, and
the circumstances, is helpful both before and during the process description.
The citizen's behavior should be clearly visible. Such questions need to be
answered as:

- How many applications for the service in question are filed on a yearly
  basis?
- Do the applications indicate a stable pattern or are there peaks
  (e.g., seasonal)?
- Is there any backlog in the process?
- Are there stocks and temporary stocks (piles on desks) at the work
  places? If so, did you count them?
- Are there customer satisfaction statistics available about the process?
- What questions do applicants ask about this process? (Do they ask for
  clarification? Are we incomplete?)
- How often do we grant the request; how often do we turn it down?
- Can a distinction be made between simple applications and more
  complex ones? What is it?

Table 4.2 Four Categories of Public Processes

Kind of Public Processes			
Variation	High	Examples: • License to demonstrate • Allocation of a new business park • Appeal procedures	Examples: • Application for a complex building permit • Dealing with complaints • Application for environmental permit
	Low	Examples: • Preparing the financial statements • The voting process • Exemptions for beekeepers	Examples: • Processing notification of damage of the public space (pothole) • Application for a passport or driver's license • Processing the mail
		Low	High
		Frequency	

- Is there much variation in the applications or the kind of service that they entail? If so, where can this variation be found?
- How is this variation proportioned? Please supply data.
- What legislation and regulation apply to this process?

Processes in the public sector may be divided into four categories (Table 4.2). Each organization decides differently which process belongs to what quadrant.

Decide to which category the process belongs. Start with a pilot of a relevant but not too complex process. For the pilot study, choose a process with high frequency and little variation.

The tools of the value stream mapper are large, legal-sized sheets, a selection of color Post-its®, and some markers. Knowledge of the current process comes from the people who work in or on the process daily. (See Chapters 6 and 7 for more on this.) Optionally, the supervisor can make an inventory of the process steps using a process analysis sheet (PAS) before the VSM session. (You will find an example of a PAS in Appendix A.)

How to Map a Value Stream

The process description starts with an empty sheet. The description starts at the top left: Who is the first to do what? (Figure 4.2). Usually the member of the public is the first to do something in the process. Sketch the VSM in as much detail as possible. Someone putting something in someone else's tray or reading documents are all process steps in their own right and, therefore, should be included in the VSM. The wastes are embedded in these details, but so is much of the improvement potential. The step-by-step plan below reflects the development of a VSM for the current state (see Figures 4.2, 4.3 and 4.1b).

- The post-its in the left column represent the players in the process
- The post-its in the row behind the player represent the actions taken by this player, in the correct sequence
- When writing the actions on a post-it, always use verbs
- Use arrows for the handovers
- In the row "action time" row, post-its are placed with the estimated time one action takes
- The "lead time" row contains the lead time per set of acts, also written on the post-its
- The triangles represent inventory (Work in Process), measured by just counting the pile of applications lying on one's desk
- The row in the middle contains examples of the used documents in the process or print screens of the software used
- Use the symbols from Table 4.3

Build the Value Stream Map from left to right and follow the route of an application. Is that all? Yes, it is a simple but very effective tool. Don't make it more complicated. Concentrate on a good discussion and fact finding.

Example: Sending a Letter of Receipt

Figure 4.2 and Figure 4.3 show the current state of the example process as described in the Chapter 3 section on "Action Time and Lead Time." Once again, a financial supervisor can fine a financial organization (such as a bank or insurance company) in case of violation. The financial organization may file a written objection against this. The supervisor should notify the organization who filed a complaint of the receipt of the complaint, after which the complaint is taken into consideration—a slow and painstaking process.

Sending a letter of receipt doesn't look like a gigantic obstacle at first glance. The complaint, however, makes a journey from the mailroom via

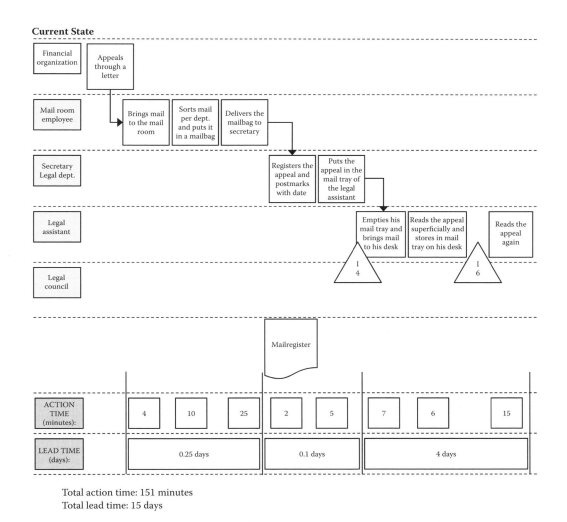

Current State

Total action time: 151 minutes
Total lead time: 15 days

Figure 4.2   The left side of the value stream of the current state map.

secretarial office to the legal assistant via the secretary, who will convert it to a confirmation of receipt, via the legal council for a signature, and back again—a process with 10 handovers and 15 days lead time.

To complete the current state, the wastes and opportunities for improvement are reflected. Every waste or opportunity for improvement is written on a Post-it® and placed on the current state (Figure 4.4 to Figure 4.6). Don't limit team discussion to identifying the wastes; discuss the sources of these wastes as well. As soon as one member considers something a waste or an opportunity for improvement, it's included in the current state without further discussion. Only when it has been put down on paper is the discussion on the future state declared open.

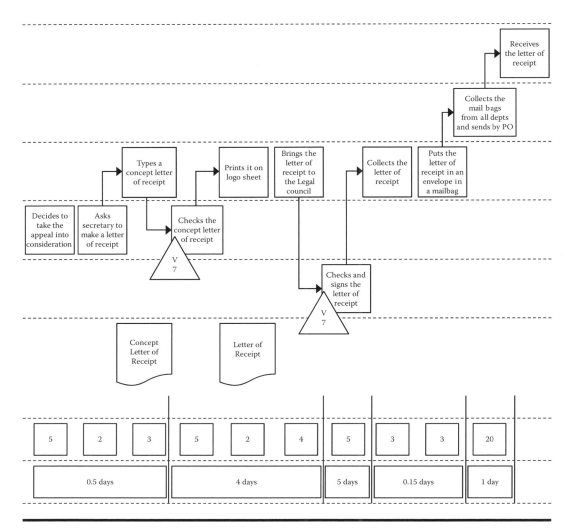

Figure 4.3   The right side of the value stream of the current state map.

Mapping the Future State

Before the new process is sketched in the future state map, the team leader asks what the ideal process should look like. How would the process run if no legal obstacles or other preconditions would stand in the way? That is, what is the ideal process as far as the individual citizen is concerned and, as far as society is concerned, the citizen collective? Obviously this process is not realistic; legal obstacles and preconditions must always be dealt with in real life. Still, this exercise is of major importance in broadening the mindsets of the parties involved. Figure 4.7 shows the ideal state of the process.

Current State

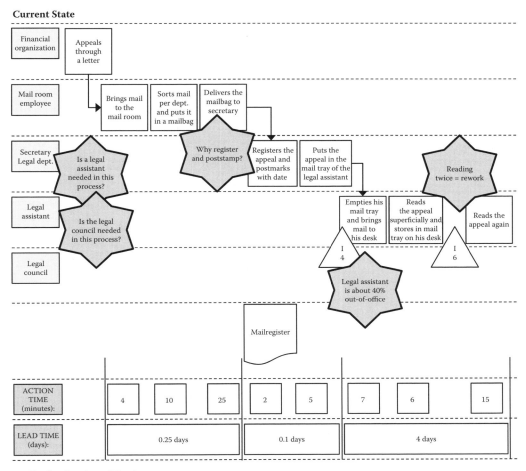

Total action time: 151 minutes
Total lead time: 15 days

Figure 4.4 The left side of the value stream of the current state map with opportunities for improvement.

Another way to get people to analyze their processes by taking a broader and more radical view is for them to be temporarily released from the reality of their process and to experience the power of the Lean principles and tools in a Lean simulation. It's a safe environment because, after all, it's not their process. Therefore, all participants can experience the Lean theory for themselves without any preconceptions or value judgments. Afterwards, with the experience behind them, the team can judge their own process and assess which Lean principles are most applicable to their own situation. For the Lean simulation, don't fall back on the all-too-familiar Lego games that are used for Lean company trainings, but use simulation games that strongly resemble the

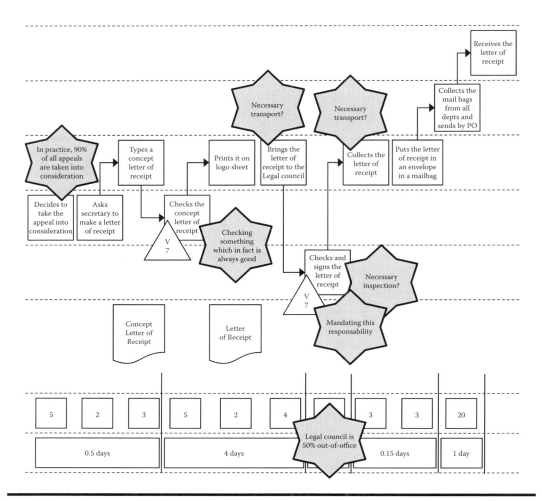

Figure 4.4   The right side of the value stream of the current state map with opportunities for improvement.

administrative processes from the public sector. This way, the simulation is not too far removed from daily practice and it is easy for participants to make the transformation from the process to the improvement assignment.

The best way is to draw the future state as close as possible to the ideal process. In this example, the ideal process is not achievable in practice because legislation does not allow automatic replies, and replies without mentioning the subject are not desirable either. In the ideal situation, the mailroom sends the letter of receipt to the financial organization. However, they are not able to distinguish the difference between letters of objection and other types of letters. This means that the secretary has to do it.

The future state map construction is similar to the current state map. Start out with clean, large sheets; the description starts top left: Who is the first to

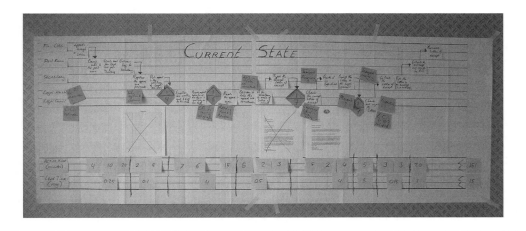

Figure 4.6   The Current State

do what? Debone the current process so that value-creating actions get all the room they need with as little deadly waste as possible. The future state can be mapped in two ways:

1. *Redesign the process such that it can be implemented in its totality and within a term decided on beforehand.*
   The process that results from this has the potential of being implemented within several months. The advantage of this approach is that it produces fast results, so there's success to be celebrated fast, too. The disadvantage is that you can't milk the process for every drop it's worth because of the time limit.
2. *Redesign the process to approach the ideal as perfectly as possible, then decide in a step-by-step plan how long implementation will take.*
   The advantage of this method is that it can potentially result in a radical redesign of the process. The implementation will take longer. In reality it can be so long that there is a decline in motivation. Experience has shown that it may yield an implementation plan of several years because new or substantially redesigned software applications are required.
   In the everyday reality of public service, information technology (IT) capacity is a major obstacle on the road to improvement.

A second disadvantage is that the implementation of some of the solutions conceived can take so long that the expected gain has by then vanished into thin air as a result of amendments of the law or other changes in the fast-changing political and legal environment.

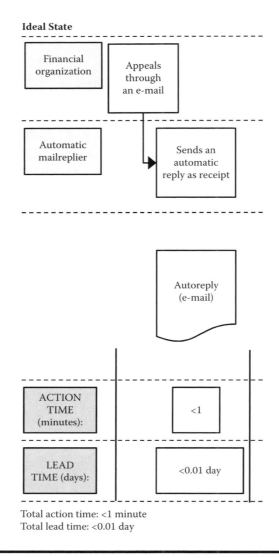

Figure 4.7   The Ideal State

The future state shows an improved process:

■ Lead time decreased from 15 to 1.5 days
■ Four instead of ten handovers
■ Action time decreased from 171 minutes to 64
■ "Expensive" minutes saved from the jurist's and legal council's time

(See Figure 4.8 and Figure 4.9 for the Future State.)

Both in the current state and in the future state map, a variety of VSM symbols can be used (Table 4.3).

Future State

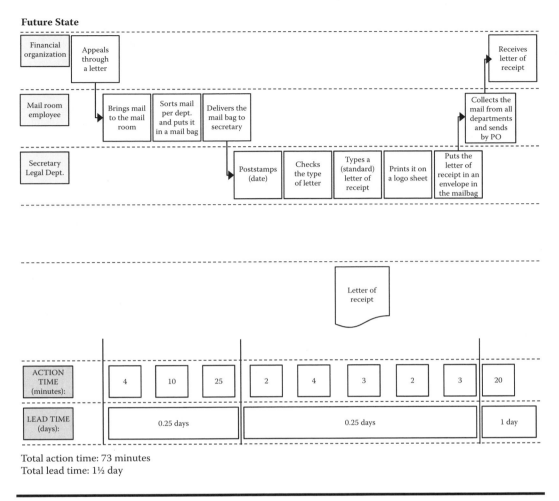

Total action time: 73 minutes
Total lead time: 1½ day

Figure 4.8   The Future State

Save the Sophisticated Tools for Later

When a public organization starts with Lean, it is common sense not to aim too high. Don't insist on the implementation of what is known as "Lean for the advanced." There are many sophisticated Lean tools and methods that are not explained in this book but that can work in the reality of the public sector. Experience with many public organizations and some commercial ones, as well, has shown that a start made with simple tools can yield considerable gain in the first few years. It's better to focus on the attitude that befits Lean. Such as it is, don't accept waste any longer, and put the citizen first. In the first startup years, tools like VSM and 5S, together with kaizen teams, will be accurate.

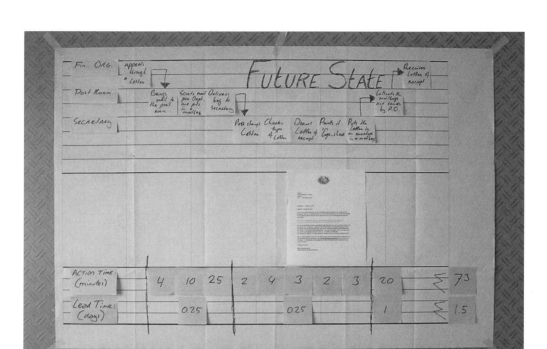

Figure 4.9

It's like picking apples from a tree. The low-hanging fruit is easy to pick without advanced instruments. The higher the fruit, the more instruments one needs. The other reason is that people tend to react negatively on long analysis sessions and sophisticated instruments. You might discourage people with them and in the end the analysis will run aground. Choose fast-action and quick results in the beginning of the Lean program.

Table 4.3 Symbols Used in Value Stream Maps

Symbol	Name	Description
△ I 25	Work in Process	Digital and analog temporary stock waiting with someone, somewhere in the workflow; the digit in the triangle represents the number of items at a specific place in stock
	Supermarket	Picking stock of, e.g., blank documents, questionnaires, and writing materials
→	Manual information stream	Translocation of physical documents
→	Electronic information stream	Electronic data transport
1-4	Kanban	Signal in the form of a kanban (ref. Chapter 5) with a minimum and maximum number of items
↻	Recovery run	Part of the process that needs to be run again due to lack of information or processing flaws
👓	Checkup	Checkups in the process and formalizing their status by means of initials or signature

Chapter 5

Flow and the Pull Principle

Strive for Continuous One-Piece Flow

When improving service, effectiveness comes before efficiency. If an organization wants to focus on the customer, it must first attain efficacy in its supply of services. Maintaining this efficacy, it can then aim for greater efficiency. This way, the problem is approached from the outside to effect change within. First focus on the public's needs, then model your organization accordingly. Note the difference. Is a manager's first question when being presented with an idea for improvement: "How does it improve the member of the public's situation?" (efficacy) or "What's it going to cost?" (efficiency).

In traditional organizations, people work on a task-oriented basis. They know what to do on a daily basis, which is to process all sorts of tasks and requests while following standards. In many cases, they are not sufficiently aware of the "customer" or of the process in its entirety. This mindset results in employees organizing their jobs around their set of tasks. They organize tasks to best fit their calendar. Their own efficiency, and that of their department, is their main focus.

When these traditional organizations want to improve, they approach the change from inside, working outwards: What is better for our organization? The result of this mindset is an efficient organization that is not very effective. This means long wait times for the applicant because it is more efficient to process certain matters once a week or because it's more efficient to open the counters mornings only, between 10 and 12 (closed on Fridays), or because it's more efficient to process applications by the pile.

If you look around in these organizations, you can see the symptoms: piles on desks and full in-trays. It's not unusual for processes with an average lead time of four weeks to contain only 20 minutes of action time and four minutes of value-creating action—i.e., 20% of the action time and as little as 0.4‰ of total lead time.

Third Stage of Lean: Create Flow

The third stage of Lean is about creating flow. Flow is achieved the moment a process runs smoothly, without fits or starts. This state is approached as soon as a large amount of waste is eliminated from the processes. Reducing the number of handovers results in a more fluid process, while eliminating checks and wait times reduces lead time. The ultimate form of flow is achieved when all temporary inventory (what is known as work in process [WIP]) has been removed and one-piece flow rules. WIP is an obstacle to achieving flow. It is generated by differences in work speed between the players in the process and by people organizing their work in a task-oriented fashion rather than in a process-oriented one.

Processes often cover several desks or departments. When each employee involved in the process works in isolation and according to batches, this can be very efficient for each single employee. But the sum of all process wait times is enormous because there is wait time to be reckoned with between all these islands (Figure 5.1). Design the new process according to the principle of *continuous flow*: Documents are no longer processed by the stack and don't land on piles, but are handed over to the next department one by one, to an employee who starts on it right away (Figure 5.2).

A continuous one-by-one flow will only work if each desk workload is adapted to the total process workload and to the public's rate of request. If in our example the person in the middle needs significantly more time for

Figure 5.1   Isolated islands: batch and queue.

Figure 5.2   One-piece flow.

Figure 5.3   Imbalance.

each product than other employees, a pile will build up to one side of him, while the person on his other side is idle every so often, awaiting input. The employee in the middle forms the constraint in this process—a matter of imbalance (Figure 5.3).

Application for Facilities: Working in Cells

An example of one-piece flow comes from the Care and Welfare Service of a large municipality. Processing requests for facilities, such as medical aids and home care, is a continuous process in many countries.

> *Applications come in all year round. The law stipulates that an applicant requesting a provision must be notified within eight weeks if the request is granted or not. The average lead time is six weeks. The department manager doesn't accept this exceptionally long lead time any longer. He has made the decision to distribute process and staff differently over this high-frequency process.*

In the current situation, the department receives and registers all applications and sends the applicant confirmation of receipt. The application is processed, the applicant is notified of the decision, and if he or she qualifies for it, the provision becomes available. The first part of the process—receiving the application and sending confirmation of receipt—hardly ever varies and does not require any legal knowledge. The second part, dealing with the application, shows some variation, and the person responsible for dealing with it needs to possess legal knowledge to come to a well-founded decision as to the granting of the request. All requests may be categorized roughly into two: simple and complex. In the current situation, simple and complex applications are integrated into the process together. Complex applications (20%) require a doctor's certificate.

For the new process, it was decided to separate the simple from the complex applications and to process them within a day. The complex applications are processed through a separate process. Two identical work cells are set up that consist of four employee stages with administrative employees and consultants: The first stage receives the applications, records them in the system, and draws up the confirmation of receipt. The second stage reads all applications and decides which ones are simple and which ones are complex. The third-stage employees consider the simple applications, and the fourth see to it that the applicant is notified of the decision. The rationale behind this is that each simple application is addressed within one day, whereby it is transferred immediately from one stage to the next as soon as it has been processed. The manager has the task to balance the four-staged process such that each stage is finished by the end of the day. Physically, the department is changed as well. In the old situation there was a hallway with separate offices for administration and consultants. Now, employees with different tasks share the same office space. Figure 5.4 and Figure 5.5 are what is known as "spaghetti diagrams," reflecting the department division before and after the change. The black lines indicate the flow of applications that travel through the process. A spaghetti diagram can be made simply with the use of a marker on a map, tracking the route of an application.

Takt Time

Inventory can result from production that is faster than customer demand. If one product is purchased daily, while you're producing ten, you produce

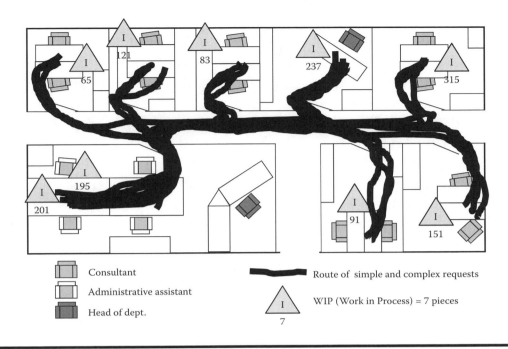

Figure 5.4   Spaghetti diagram of Current State.

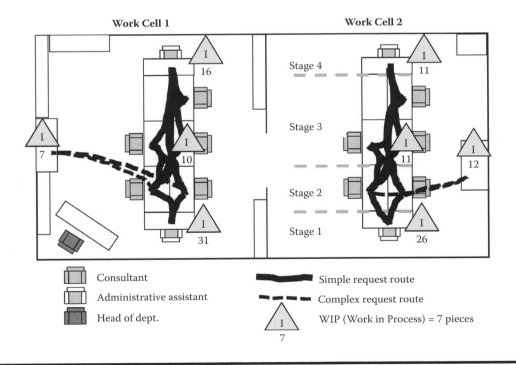

Figure 5.5   Spaghetti diagram of Future State.

a ten-day inventory. Inventory is one of the eight deadly wastes. If you produce to customer demand, you would have to produce one every day. The rate at which the customer purchases products is what is known as takt time. The German word *takt* means rhythm, in the sense of a director using his baton to indicate an orchestra's tempo.

Now, that makes for a good story in the industry, but how does it apply to administrative processes in the government? In the example, takt time can be calculated. However, takt time is not the rate at which the customer purchases products, but the rate at which the application for facilities come in. Say that 50 applications arrive each working day. A working day consists of 450 minutes, so each stage has to deal with a "product" every 9 minutes.

$$\text{Takt time} = \frac{\text{Available mean working time daily}}{\text{Mean number of applications daily}} = \frac{450}{50} = 9$$

If an employee from stage 1 needs on average 8.5 minutes for receipt and recording of each application, then one employee is needed for the job. The cycle time of stage 1 is then eight and a half minutes. A stage 2 employee spends an average of 14 minutes per application to decide which application is simple and which is complex. This 14-minute cycle time is more than the 9-minute takt time. That is why two persons are necessary in this unit to keep up with the rate of applications. In that case, the cycle time of this stage is 14 divided by 2 = 7 minutes. Each seven minutes this stage delivers an application ready to be processed by the next stage.

The work in stage 3 takes the most time. The processing of a simple application takes 30 minutes on average. This means that four employees are needed in stage 3 to keep up with the rate. However, only the simple applications end up with this team and approximately 80% of the applications are classified as simple by stage 2. That is 40 out of a daily 50. The takt time of the simple requests is 450/40 = 11.3 minutes. If the manager puts three employees to work in stage 3, the average cycle time is 30/3 = 10 minutes. That is slightly under takt time, and, therefore, enough to keep up with the process rate. The employee in stage 4 only requires 7 minutes per application. It fits well into the takt process.

After the first week of working with the new system, the picture is shown in Figure 5.6.

Stage 1 does not get the job done within takt time. The estimation that the job can be done within 8.5 minutes has been too optimistic. The

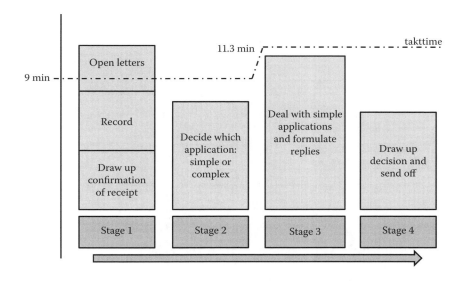

Figure 5.6   Balance diagram.

employee needs on average 10 minutes per application, as it turns out. The other three stages can keep up just fine. Stage 4 even has too much wait time; the cycle turns out to be at maximum 6.5 minutes per application. The manager might at this point decide to put one extra member of staff on stage 1. The staff points out that if applicants receive a reply quickly, they may forego the confirmation of receipt altogether. Confirmation of receipt and reply (decision) can be included in a single letter. However, this implies that the confirmation of receipt for complex applications cannot be drawn up before the distinction between simple and complex has been made. The stage 4 employee has so much time to spare that he can take on drafting confirmations of receipt for the complex applications. The balance would then look like what is shown in Figure 5.7.

The result is a well-balanced process with practically no WIP at any stage at the end of each working day. Slight variations in input are normal. The manager uses the true number of applications to estimate the number of staff for each stage. During the course of a day the manager can tell from the workload in all stages and the formation of WIP if there is balance and react accordingly with staff transfer.

One-Day Flow

Striving for one-piece flow is only possible for high-frequency processes with a reasonably stable customer demand and little variation in application

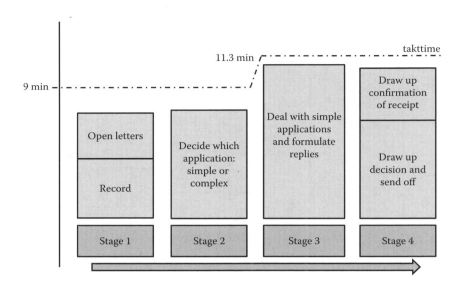

Figure 5.7 Balance diagram.

processing time. When variation is greater, one-day flow is preferable to one-piece flow. This means that every employee partaking in the process must move his daily inventory onto the next person in the process at the end of the day. The next working day will present a similar workload for another working day.

Pull Principle

The fourth stage of Lean is about working according to the pull principle. This means agreeing to produce nothing until there's demand for the product. The supplying department only sets out to produce something when the receiving department asks for it. This way, a product is pulled through a process. The pull principle has a number of advantages:

■ There is minimal or no intermediate inventory (no WIP). A department does not create product before a request has arrived from the receiving department.
■ The process is clear due to lack of intermediate inventory.
■ Imbalance in the process becomes very clear when the supplying departments, working at higher speed than the receiving department, show idle capacity.
■ The process lead time is decidedly shorter.

The pull principle could be introduced in the example in section "Takt Time" by placing three trays between each stage, all of which may contain no more than one application. The moment a stage 3 employee removes an application from a tray for processing, this is a signal to stage 2 to fill the tray.

Kanban

Flow is a process that can be more fully elaborated with a kanban system. Kanban (Japanese for "visible record" or "signboard") is a stocking system used to guarantee that in the sequence of previous and following process steps everyone is always provided with a sufficient supply of current tasks and support material. A kanban can take the form of an order slip, but it also can be a tray that holds no more that a set amount of work. The three trays we mentioned above are an example of kanban.

> *A scene in a bar serves as a simple illustration of a kanban system. A customer is very thirsty and wants to be served his favorite drink without fail, but without constantly having to order. So, he has made a delivery deal with the bartender: There shall be two full glasses on the bar. When he's finished one, he shoves it to the back and starts on the second, which is full. The empty glass serves as a kanban signal to the bartender, who removes it, and replaces it with a full one. This way, the customer decides the rate of delivery (pouring). When the rate varies, no large stock build-ups or thirsty shortfalls result. In this bar, a pull principle has been generated to guide a simple process, using kanban. The barman does not build a large stock of drinks but delivers only when the customer gives the signal—an empty glass.*

Overly large WIP reflects a lack of balance in the process flow. Use kanbans to ensure that employees do not deliver before they have been given the kanban for it.

Con WIP

In the public sector, there are many processes with too much variation for useful implementation of kanban systems. In order to ensure flow in processes, given that variation, it may be necessary to streamline the

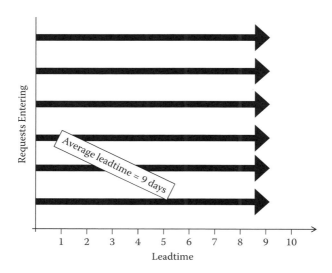

Figure 5.8   All of the requests enter the process instantly.

customer demand at the beginning of the process. A methodology for streamlining is con WIP (constant work in process). Con WIP is based on the principle that the processing of a highly irregular supply of new applications must be regulated to a constant work flow. The number of applications being processed remains constant regardless of the variation in supply. Don't start with everything at once, but set a maximum number of applications that may be processed simultaneously. This principle, although it sounds contradictory, reduces lead time. Take the following situation:

Version A

A group of employees receives six applications to process simultaneously. They start to deal with all of these applications at once. The average lead time per application in this version is nine days (Figure 5.8).

Version B (The Con WIP Alternative)

The con WIP alternative is for the same group of employees to start dealing with two of the six applications, and to leave the other four for the time being. Because the employees are only working on two instead of six applications, they are finished earlier. The lead time of the two applications is three days. Only when the first two applications have been completed are the next two processed. These two applications are completed after three days wait time, plus

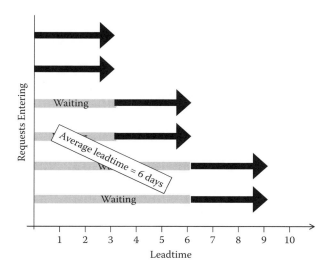

Figure 5.9   Requests enter the process two by two.

three days process time, a sum of six days. The processing of the last two applications starts only after a wait time of six days. The sum of the wait time for the purchasers of the final two applications is therefore a six-day wait + three days of processing = nine days. The average lead time of this version, however, is six days, and that is three days shorter (33%) than version A (Figure 5.9).

Con WIP is a fine method if the following criteria are met.

■ Stick to the first in, first out principle: Applications that come in first are dealt with first. If you don't apply the FIFO principle, lead time will appear to have a lot of variation for the purchaser.

■ Everyone sticks to the agreed constant WIP cap. In the current example, never process more or fewer than two applications at once. To maintain the WIP cap, exits from the process trigger starts in the process.

■ Actual lead time will only shorten once there isn't a single application lying around waiting somewhere in the process. The applications are constantly being dealt with; the employees have no other activities going on than dealing with the two applications.

■ The process has no rework; whatever has been dealt with smoothly flows downstream, not upstream.

The basic principle says that when demand is fluctuating, it's better to have limited WIP in the process and leave the rest of the applications waiting at the gate of the process (Figure 5.10) instead of letting them all into the

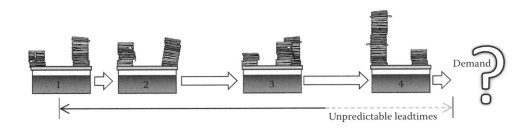

Figure 5.10   All requests enter the process instantly.

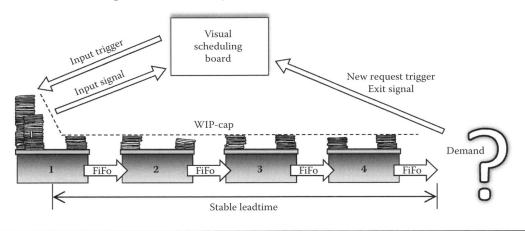

Figure 5.11   Con WIP situation.

process (Figure 5.11). Under con WIP, a job will not be started unless a place in the system has been vacated for it. The flow, not the capacity is balanced.

The benefits of this system include:

■ Because the number of applications in the process is constant, one can predict the lead time.
■ It gives a constant workload for the involved employees, which leads to less stress.
■ It gives the planner the opportunity to give priority to specific orders.

It is important with con WIP that the agreed WIP cap is in line with the average number of applications. Use Little's law to calculate this WIP cap:

$$\text{WIP capacity} = \text{Lead time target} \times \text{completion rate}$$

$$\left[\# \text{ things}\right] = \left[\text{days}\right] \times \left[\# \text{ things/day}\right]$$

An example:

> *The target lead time of a process is four days. The completion rate, the number of applications that may be completed daily, is 20. The WIP cap has been set to 80 items (4 × 20). The process as a whole should never contain more than 80 items WIP. If there are more than 80, the supply should be stopped temporarily. If there are fewer than 80, there is idle capacity and new applications should enter the process quickly.*

The *average* takt time of this process is 20 applications per day. The number of applications fluctuates, but the agreed WIP remains at 80. Application waiting time will increase temporarily when input is increased because the applications are lying around for longer before they are addressed. If the input's average rate increases (and thereby takt time), the process owner has to decide if he will accept a longer lead time or utilize extra capacity. A computer program or a plan board (Figure 5.12 and Figure 5.13) can support visual control of the constant flow.

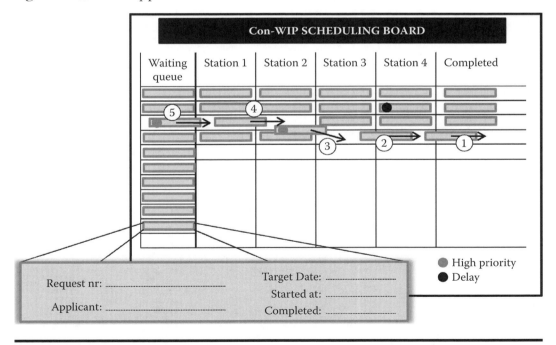

Figure 5.12   Con WIP scheduling board.

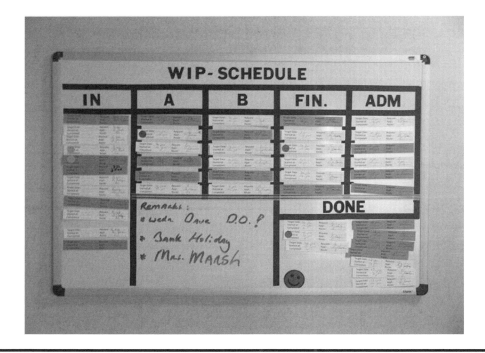

Figure 5.13   Photo of a WIP schedule.

Mono Processes

Handovers are responsible for the duration of lead times. The more handovers, the longer the wait time for the public. There is no scientific proof of this (yet), but you could use the following rule of thumb: If n is the number of staff playing an active role in a process, then n^2 is the number of days lead time. So, four employees ($n = 4$) make the number of lead time days for any service 16. If one person was responsible for the service ($n = 1$), he or she would have had the job done in one day (Figure 5.14).

Processes without handovers are ideal in certain situations. It simply means that one person handles the entire process. These mono processes

Figure 5.14   Isolated islands: batch and queue.

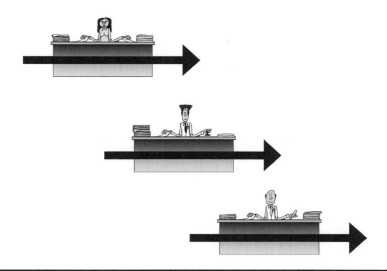

Figure 5.15 Mono processes.

work optimally if the staff sticks to the same principles as those of the con WIP: follow the FIFO principle, process only one application at a time, and don't perform any other activities in the meantime. Of course, not all processes can be mono processes—sometimes the knowledge required is too specific and you get too much of the eighth deadly waste: insufficient use of talents. A process that consists of 80% administrative work and 20% legal deliberation can't be completed by an administrative employee alone because he or she does not have the legal knowledge required. However, a lawyer doing all the work would not be able to put his or her legal skills to sufficient use.

In Figure 5.14, all tasks of one single process are distributed in order among three employees. The disadvantage of this system is that it creates three wait times. Each transition creates an initial start-up waste, plus there is a higher risk of faulty communication and errors. Improving cycle time of one of the three tasks creates little profit; the process will only run more smoothly if the profit is realized in all three tasks. In Figure 5.15, all tasks of the same process are performed by one employee. The wait times are minimized because there are no handovers and there is hardly a chance of faulty communication because very little internal communication is required.

Push in the Public Sector

In administrative processes in the public sector, hardly any traditional push situations occur, such as when companies produce on a forecast based, in turn, on historical demand. A classic example of push in the public sector is building new houses or residential sections on the basis of a forecast of the chances that people will want to live there. This can turn out to be a big disappointment, resulting in vacancy.

Most public processes do not start before a member of the public demands something: the pull principle. But, inside the processes, there often is push—staff that have finished some process of internal action and push their inventory of completed tasks onto the next person in the process.

A well-known example of push in government organizations is the overwhelming political ambition expressed in policy, weighed against the limited capacity of the civil service organization to program and implement all of this policy. In practically all government organizations, the executive capacity demanded by all governmental ambitions far exceeds the actual capacity to complete the policies. This is the result of politicians piling policy on top of policy. Nothing is prioritized. Everything has to be done and done at once. Piling resolution upon resolution, promise on promise is what draws votes. However, if you want everything, you will never have enough money and definitely not enough civil service capacity. As a result, a share of the plans is moved on until next year, which in its turn is already filled to the brim with ambitious plans. Politicians would show more leadership by being more selective and not try to implement so much policy, but dare to end some, too.

Sometimes Push Is Better

Because of its public duty, the government is sometimes faced with situations where a push system is inevitable or simply better than a pull system from a service point of view. It depends, among other things, on the role the citizen plays. The citizen subjects receive fines without asking for them, and the citizen taxpayers receive tax assessments. These are typical examples of push. Getting "services" from the government is not always a voluntary thing. A member of the public does not want to go for a building permit, he *has* to do so (push). But, no permits are lying around waiting for customer demand (pull). There is no inventory of permits.

The citizen, as a government customer, is sometimes better off if the government utilizes push, not pull. A municipality may have created provisions for people living below the poverty line. In addition to other provisions, these people are entitled to partial or complete remission of local taxes. The municipality has estimated the number of local residents entitled to this service. The municipality is aware of the financial position of this target group because it is by and large the same group already registered with the social services and receiving welfare. Financial reports show, time and again, that half the money set aside for them is never used. It turns out that a maximum of 50% of the residents entitled to this service make use of it. When the target group is investigated, it turns out that many people aren't aware of the service, don't realize they qualify, or are ashamed to apply. All the while the services are extensively publicized.

If the government considers promoting the public's welfare as one of its most important tasks and thinks that everyone entitled to services and remissions should receive them, then in some cases waiting for customer demand is not enough. The municipality in question in this example chose for push. A member of the public entitled to remission of local taxes gets remission, no questions asked—an example of delivery without explicit customer demand.

A fine example of the push principle comes from the Dutch municipality of Eindhoven (population 215,000). Everyone aged 75 and older gets offered a free two hours of domestic help weekly, without request. This gives the municipality more information about their needs and, to the surprise of many, this investment has resulted in an unexpected cutback in costs. In total, this group now uses fewer care facilities than before. For those who can't or won't come to the local government offices because it's too much of a barrier or because they have no clear knowledge of what sort of support is available, the municipality reaches out to the community. A team of specially trained professionals can deliver closer to home, or even at home, the same services as at the local office counter.

The Road to Flow and Pull

You don't get flow in your processes just like that. Some improvement steps must precede it. It can even be dangerous to move on to flow and apply the pull principle at the very start of Lean. You won't get flow into a process if it's still filled to the brim with deadly waste. Bumpy processes are the result of wastes, such as checks, defects, and rework. Flow is blocked by people multitasking. If employees have tasks in several processes simultaneously, what happens is that their focus gets shifted away from the processes and onto the efficient planning of their own tasks and jobs. People will organize their work to fit their own calendar and not that of the processes geared to the public.

In addition, public processes are often not fit for principles such as flow and pull. An application for a building permit for a big project is not a simple process of ordered logical steps in short succession. Parties, such as housing co-ops and property developers, applying for such permits have to hand over concrete building plans, drawings included. Having these drafted is very expensive. So, the parties don't rush matters, but request time to develop and reflect. Government and property developer often take time for this creative process, and sometimes it can take up to a few years without this causing irritation on either side.

Another reason why processes can't always come to ultimate flow is the processes' low frequency. Some processes are asleep so much of the time that it really is not worth the trouble to make them Lean.

If you start with Lean in your organization, for the first years concentrate on removing waste from processes. Make sure that all employees learn to look at their work with a keen eye for waste. Look for basic stability. Flow and pull will follow later.

Chapter 6

Mobilize Employees

Ownership

When managers mingle, it's only a matter of time before the term *empowerment* is heard, at which point everyone starts nodding their heads deeply and sagely. Is it just "words, words, words" or are employees really getting involved? For illustration, see what happens when they come up with ideas for improvement. "I involve all my people in process improvements" sounds really good. But, how exactly do you do that? Do you give your employees free reign to come up with ideas for service improvement, and then put them into practice?

No Head

In many traditional organizations, thought and action are still two separate entities. The people at the top have large heads and no hands—it's where all the head work is done. The operational and support staff have no head, but only a pair of large hands—they are responsible for keeping the organization running (Figure 6.1). In organizations with traditional leadership, the main impression is that employees have to leave their brain at the gate before they are allowed in to work. Managers are employed to solve problems, and the remaining personnel perform the grunt work. When it comes to solving problems, managers in the public sector sometimes put more faith in subcontracted staff than in their own. Managers of such organizations overlook one important phenomenon. Performance depends for an important part

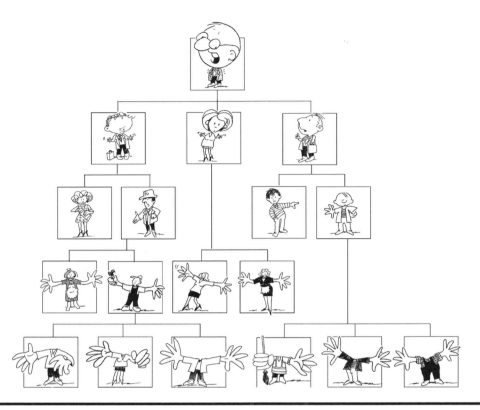

Figure 6.1

on motivation, and motivation of employees has a direct link with owner-ship. Ownership is the feeling that an employee gets when he is able and permitted to exert influence on his own work. In practice, this means that the employee identifies any obstacles that he faces on the job, generates solutions, and tries them out to solve the problem.

People do not readily accept solutions that are imposed on them, whereas solutions generated by people themselves are accepted automatically. Say a solution is found in a change of work method. The success of this solution does not depend solely on the quality of this new work method. If the new work method is not accepted, it won't be implemented either.

People often oppose solutions that they have not come up with themselves. They do not feel that they own these solutions. This feeling is even stronger when solutions are thought up by a staff service, or even worse, by external consultants. The chances that these solutions will be broadly based are not very good. Sometimes it's difficult enough to sell the solutions to your own colleagues. It's much better if people involved in the process perform the analysis themselves and generate the solutions.

Should Work Be Fun?

Is it important that people enjoy their work? Should work be fun? There are those who suggest that support staff mainly work for the money. This is particularly true with temporary staff, who, to begin with, are regarded as a lower species. No one ever expects them to show commitment to the job: "They're only in it for the money." A sales director of a packaging manufacturer once said, "Isn't it a bit passé saying that work should be fun, too? It's a business relationship, right?"

A happiness study conducted by the Randstad employment agency (2005) found that more than 50% of the respondents felt that work brings happiness and a sense of fulfillment. Fewer than 20% felt it did not. People working full time dedicate approximately one-third of their waking hours to work, undeniably a large portion of their lives.

On what does a working person's happiness depend? Salary? A study conducted by a labor union (FNV, 2005) found that salary is not in the top 10 reasons for work satisfaction. A good salary is, at best, a reason *not* to be *unhappy*. Happiness at work comes from the right atmosphere, the task content, and the level of independence to do the job. Invest in this top three and chances are that you will motivate your staff and increase performance in the process.

Organizations that regard personnel as people who get paid to perform set tasks sacrifice unused capacity. As a result, employees mainly apply their talents outside their jobs (e.g., as members of committees or investment clubs or doing volunteer work).

Managers sometimes find it hard to imagine that you can be happy with a daytime job of dealing with applications or payroll processing. In everyday practice, these are under-appreciated tasks. An employee of a fax department once said: "The guys at the Urban Redevelopment Department get a round of applause for every new sexy little project, but at the Bureau of Population Affairs or the Tax Department, we never get that."

The processes of population affairs and tax collecting are considered tedious and simple. But the people performing these tasks on a daily basis regard these processes as interesting and complex, and they know a lot about them. For them, this work offers ample discussion material.

It's a wonderful opportunity to improve the organization's performance. Good performance depends strongly on motivation. Motivation of staff has a direct link with ownership. Ownership is the feeling that an employee gets when he is able and permitted to exert influence on his work. In practice, this means that the employee identifies the obstacles that he faces on the job, generates solutions, and tries them out to solve the problems. Employees enjoy discussing work-related content, and they enjoy wielding influence on it in order to make processes run more smoothly. Dare to give them the room to improve their work themselves. This way you create ownership for the solutions. Look for consensus for existing problems, but leave solutions to the employees.

Suggestion Box

Some managers read books about leadership and become convinced that employees need to be involved in process improvement. Ownership must be stimulated. One attempt to that effect is the system of the suggestion box. A few suggestion boxes are distributed around the building, and a suggestion box committee is created. The staff is invited to write down and submit ideas for improvement, and the ideas, if implemented, are financially compensated. Managers are happy to receive a measly 20 ideas a year for every 100 employees. However, there is no guarantee that a submitted idea will be implemented. The idea committee decides if an idea is feasible and effective and should be rewarded.

The committee is headed by managers. Once again the big heads ultimately decide if an idea is any good, even though it was submitted by an employee with 15 years experience on the job, for which he or she now had a good suggestion.

In addition, with this suggestion reward system, the manager implies that submitting improvement ideas is something so exceptional it should be financially rewarded—i.e., "We will buy your ideas." What the employee really wants is for improvement to be part of the job.

In most organizations it takes ages to hear what's happening to a suggestion someone submitted. Small wonder that most suggestion boxes anywhere are filled with chewed-down apples and pellets of indistinct origin.

Power of Thought and Power of Action

Leadership is not about suggesting solutions and improvement ideas yourself. You are not the Great Improver. And neither is it about deciding if an idea submitted by an employee is substantive or not. Skilled managers decide in collaboration with their employees *what* must be improved. The employees suggest ideas on *how* things can be made better: the solutions. The manager decides beforehand what preconditions these solutions must meet.

Preconditions might relate to the time frame in which the costs of the solution must be recovered. You're a good manager when you can guarantee that all solutions that meet the preconditions will be implemented, without fail.

Organizations that practice this sort of leadership have been producing more than ten implemented improvement ideas per employee per year, to great success. And what's more, employees don't just get involved in the processes, they consider themselves owners of these processes. The improvement organization does not rest on the managers alone, but in the thinking power of the employees. A true leader can tell the difference between the *what* and the *how* and leaves conceiving and executing solutions to the creativity of the employees.

Improvement in Kaizen Teams

Some problems can be addressed by individuals, while others are better suited to be addressed by a team. Improving in team formation often takes more time, but sometimes it's the best approach—for example, when a broad basis for solutions is required, or simply because two heads (or more) are better than one.

To properly analyze and improve the processes, sufficient knowledge of current processes and products is required. In most organizations knowledge of these fields is distributed among employees of different departments and disciplines, particularly if the processes are cross-departmental.

Interdepartmental teams offer a mix of knowledge and experience that exceeds that of a single person. Staff services have a wealth of knowledge about the correctness of a particular work process, but their perception of practice is less clear than that of employees working in the process on a day-to-day basis. Improving processes, therefore, is best addressed in teams consisting of a multidisciplinary mix of employees working in the processes, completed with staff service personnel.

A kaizen team is such a multidisciplinary group working on the solutions to concrete problems in the actual work field for a relatively short period. Members of the kaizen team all exert influence on the problem, directly or indirectly. The Japanese word *kaizen* translates roughly as *continuous improvement*.

When initiating a kaizen team, effective use is made of the knowledge, experience, and creativity of the employees at all levels of an organization. In this way, the quality of processes, products, and services can be improved. Working in kaizen teams and exerting influence on the quality and efficacy of your own work is an enriching experience for employees. This makes kaizen teams meaningful for the organization and employees. A kaizen team is a powerful tool to achieve acceptance of solutions. The sponsor decides *what* needs to be addressed and formulates the assignment. The team decides *how* the problem needs to be addressed and comes up with the solutions.

Dividing the Roles in Kaizen Teams

The success of a kaizen team is determined to a large extent by the team composition in relation to the subject. Have the right people been selected for the subject at hand? How have the roles been divided? Is the group large enough? Is it too large? Is there sufficient knowledge of the subject in the team?

Cooperation is making a mutual effort to achieve a particular goal. The model in Figure 6.2 describes which components are absolutely necessary for efficient cooperation in kaizen teams.

Content is the content-based discussion of the chosen subject, the exchange of facts and experiences relating to the topic.

Process is the play of mutual interactions. Are people listening to each other? Are participants helping each other? Is the atmosphere open or closed? Do the team members think it's fun/useful? Is everyone actively involved? Are there unwanted subgroups?

Procedure is about role division in the team, the following of the eight steps of the improvement cycle (see Chapter 7), and applying the correct method to map the process, plus making and living up to clear agreements.

In the model, we distinguish between the team members' role and this team leader's role.

Role of the Kaizen Leader

The leader of the kaizen team is the one who sets his compass for the team's efficacy. He keeps his eye on the group process, the process under

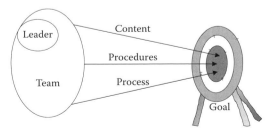

Figure 6.2   The role of the kaizen leader.

consideration, and the procedure, leaving the discussion of content to the team members.

However, a well-known pitfall for any kaizen leader is the lure of the content; a leader may at some point start interfering here. As a result, the leader may lose sight of the group process and procedure. If in daily practice the team leader is also the team members' manager, he can wield his natural authority and get team members to opt for his solutions. That's an unwanted effect.

The team leader is preeminently the one who can raise the critical "why" questions. His strongest weapons are the "why," "what," "when," "who" and "how" questions: Why do you do it like this? Why do you run checks here? What do you mean by that? When will this happen/does this happen? Who hands the document to you? How often does this happen? How many applications do you deal with?

The team leader tries to exert influence on the thought process using these questions but makes sure he does not load the team members' choice of solutions. He can encourage the team to take a critical approach to its own process. The leader of the kaizen team regularly reports to the sponsor on the progress made.

When the kaizen leader knows about the subject, the leader finds it hard to stay out of the conversation. But it is not the leader's job to be part of the discussion. This becomes even more difficult when everybody, including the team members, knows that the leader knows a lot about the subject. Choose leaders on the basis of competences in the field of team coaching. They must have an ear for what is said and what remains unspoken inside the teams and intervene accordingly. Preferably, you should not select instrumentalists for this role. They love their tools and are not always adequate in coaching teams.

Role of the Kaizen Team Members

For participation in kaizen teams, employees are invited to join who deal with a given subject on a daily basis. When participants feel committed to a subject or problem, they are more likely to seriously apply themselves to it. Participation in a team may be voluntary, but it's not noncommittal.

The task of team members is to apply their knowledge and experience to the field of the selected subject. Their role consists for the most part of delivering content. The right mix of people with enough knowledge and insight to solve the problem offers a good chance of success. A team that has been set up to reduce lead time in welfare payments would consist of consultants, an employee from the administration, and, if necessary, a quality assurance officer. A team that wants to tackle the waiting time at the counter might consist of three counter employees and a quality assurance employee.

An additional positive spin-off of kaizen teams is that team members learn improvement techniques that they can apply to their daily work as well.

Group Size

The minimum size of a kaizen team is four. With less than four members, the team is vulnerable in case one of the members drops out for some reason. More members can result in more knowledge on the subject. However, there is a maximum. In larger groups, there is a chance that some members do not participate in discussions. To ensure the active participation of all members in discussions, the maximum group size should be seven.

When assembling the team, the sponsor must take into consideration whether there is sufficient knowledge in the team to solve the problem. The innovative character of the solutions depends on the creativity of the participants. If smart solutions are available that are being applied in another organization, the sponsor may choose to add an employee from this organization to his team.

Teams concerned with improving chain processes are assembled from representatives of various organizations in the chain, including clients.

Role of the Sponsor

In traditional organizations, the direct manager acts as the Great Problem Solver. Employees are encouraged to take all work-related problems to their manager, which suggests that he will solve these problems, one and all.

A kaizen team, however, is given a problem and asked to submit solutions to the sponsor. When solutions are well thought out and substantiated, the sponsor provides the resources that the team utilizes to implement the solutions. For the sponsor, it is of major importance that he's clear about his objective. Why does he want to set up a kaizen team and what are his expectations? And why this particular subject? The main point for him is getting the team to *buy* the problem he wants to see solved.

Preconditions

The sponsor stipulates the field for the team to work in by specifying preconditions. These preconditions define borders within which the team moves and may be related to integrity and efficiency.

Examples of preconditions include:

Maximum budget
Should be feasible with current formation
Must utilize current registration system of basic facts
The customer has one contact point only
The kaizen team must operate within the framework of an existing policy
    plan and legal constraints

Preconditions can be political, economical (financial), social, or technical, or touch on legislation and the environment (e.g., ecology or the number of square feet).

Consider the type of solutions you would like to avoid, and prevent these with a well-formulated precondition. Some examples include: Are costly solutions unwanted? The precondition might then be a maximum budget of $1,000. Public organizations have hundreds of software applications in all sorts of sizes. If you, the sponsor, think that this is enough for the time being, make sure you prevent the purchase of yet another application with a solid precondition.

To avoid the fear the kaizen team will change policy, consider setting a precondition to prevent policy changes. The kaizen team will change the process, but not the policy.

The sponsor guarantees all preconditions to make a kaizen team successful. He selects a subject that fits the targets of the organization. With an eye on the subject, he selects participants for the team who feel they *own* the subject. While selecting participants, the sponsor weighs the right mix of skills of the team members, so the problem may be tackled. This may include, in addition to knowledge and experience, collaborative skills and the ability to exert a positive influence on colleagues in their own departments.

If the sponsor determines that there is not enough knowledge on a particular subject within the organization, he may decide to add an external expert to the team. This expert can introduce all sorts of new methods and ideas about which the organization knows little. This way the sponsor creates the opportunity to look beyond solutions that are too obvious.

The sponsor provides the resources, such as time and money, and may exert influence when the kaizen team faces resistance from within the organization. He also guarantees that any solution that meets the preconditions will be executed without fail. The sponsor should preferably not overrule any solutions chosen by the group that meet the preconditions. If he does, chances are that the team will withdraw from the assignment. "Do it yourself, if you're that smart."

The influence of the sponsor on the success of the team is mostly due to solid preparation. To obtain a considerable level of certainty that generated solutions are of a high quality, the leader assembles a team with sufficient knowledge of the process in which the subject is embedded, plus the skills to properly analyze it. A clear project letter with concrete preconditions, plus the correct team composition as to knowledge and the ability to work together, can prevent a kaizen team from generating problems that are off target. An example of a project letter may be found in Appendix B.

Everyday Lean

It's not hard to start with Lean, but it's hard to keep it up. How can you make sure that Lean has staying power in an organization and that Lean becomes a fixed and natural part of everyday business? Sometimes Lean can start at the bottom of an organization, when someone from middle management independently introduces it in his own department. This can definitely generate success. However, the chance that it will continue to exist depends on whether the management or the board adopts this Lean thinking and turns it into a leading principle within the organization.

The start and maintenance of organization-wide Lean vision is top-down. The organization decision makers will have to make sure that Lean remains a part of its policy. Of course, it's helpful when, for example, a mayor, members of the council, and other managers consider Lean philosophy an indispensable paradigm for the optimal performance of the organization.

Public organizations showing Lean as a fixed element of management have achieved this through:

Achieving success and sharing it organization-wide.
An improvement program constantly needs to prove its right to exist. Make sure you get that proof and that it is communicated across the organization—e.g., through Lean bulletins and an intranet site. Don't forget to put successful teams in the limelight.
Having managers stick to the Lean principles.
Many employees at the start of Lean nourish an attitude of "seeing is believing." They weren't born yesterday. How can they tell that Lean is

not just another flavor-of-the-month management game? The management should stick to the rules and principles of Lean. Specifically, if you promise that anything a kaizen team comes up with that meets the preconditions will be embedded, make good on that promise. But also stick to Lean principles in daily practice. The Lean philosophy puts the customer first. Managers who practice what they preach show the Lean attitude and make Lean decisions.

Training their employees (tools, yes, but attitude and skills first).

Train employees in Lean thinking and Lean tools. Lean thinking, in particular, is important. Employees who don't put the public first and want to create maximum value develop designs that may be good for the organization, but not for the public. It's definitely worth the trouble to train the tools as well, but limit yourself to tools that can be applied immediately and forego the abstruse techniques that don't come into play until operational management has almost been perfected. Don't turn your employees into instrumentalists.

Installing a Lean coordination team.

Install a coordination team to keep an eye on all developments inside an organization in the field of improvement and Lean. Their first task is to guard the methodology and supply advice and tools. Their second task is making Lean organization-wide. Note, however, that subjects for kaizen teams come from line management and board. They decide, in line with the organization strategy, which processes or services are ready to be improved. The board decides and guards the bigger picture as sponsor of the Lean program. This is also the place where the choice must be made how time savings will be capitalized on.

Furnishing a tracking center.

The Lean coordination team uses a specially furnished room where kaizen events can take place and where presentations and training sessions can be given. Such tracking centers are often full of presentations of recently successful teams.

Using embedded Lean practitioners.

You can choose to have external consultants supervise all kaizen and 5S events. It's preferable, however, to ensure that the organization itself has all required knowledge and skills. And, I mean, not just the tools. Choose for the role of embedded Lean practitioners people who are good, or can be good, at enthusing others. They must possess the skills to notice signs of resistance, overcome these, and to get the most from the teams. These are competencies other than making a good value stream map.

Starting kaizen events regularly.
The coordination team has to make sure that kaizen events start on a
regular basis. Subjects galore! Ensure a smooth flow in the events,
but don't go overboard. The greater the number of teams that operate
simultaneously, the longer they will take for their assignment. Avoid too
many teams in parallel, but have them operate in sequence.
*Using tools to stimulate small improvements and everyday Lean, such as
an improvement board.*

Improvement Board

Stimulate and maintain continuous improvement by constantly asking for
improvement ideas, using the Improvement Suggestions found in Appendix D.
Working with an improvement board (Figure 6.3) is a way of creating flow in
dealing with improvement proposals. Flow is regulated, as the improvement
board only holds so many suggestions, limiting the number that can be dealt
with simultaneously.

How the Suggestion Board Operates

New improvement suggestions are hung up in spiral folders to the left.
The spaces in the middle of the board are the suggestions being processed

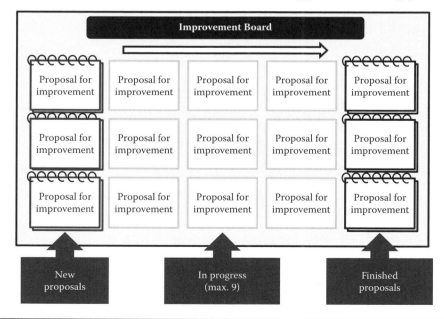

Figure 6.3   Improvement board.

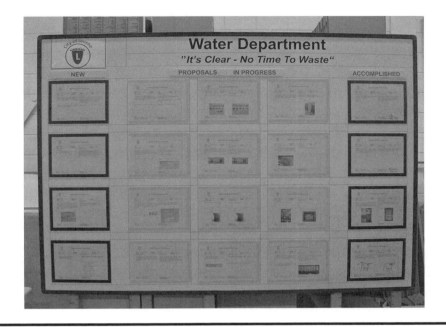

Figure 6.4   Photo of suggestion board.

(in our example, nine is the maximum). As soon as a suggestion is completed, it's moved to a spiral folder to the right. A new space is created for a new proposal (Figure 6.4).

Employees decide for their team what the priority and feasibility of each suggestion is. For each proposal: It is only completed when the person who submitted it is satisfied with the result.

Chapter 7

Continuous Improvement with Kaizen Teams

The kaizen teams use a structured approach when resolving problems or improving work processes. This structured approach requires that people first consider the scope and the main causes of the problem; only at a later stage do they start considering solutions. In addition, the procedure provides for a variety of methods to facilitate the process of describing, investigating, and resolving the problem. A kaizen team works on the basis of the cycle of improvement, which provides structure in resolving a particular problem or improving a particular process. Based on this structured approach, the team sets out to tackle the problem in an effective and action-oriented way. The core of the cycle of improvement is based on the Plan-Do-Check-Act (PDCA) cycle developed by Dr. W. Edwards Deming. Below is a brief explanation of the four phases of the PDCA cycle:

Planning phase—During this phase, the problem is considered (that is, its size and scope, frequency, causes, and impact are all assessed) and solutions are developed. The results of the Planning phase represent an analysis of the process or problem, identification of the root causes of errors and wastes, and development of an action plan containing specific solutions.

In order to achieve this result, five steps are completed:

1. The sponsor selects the subject.
2. The sponsor sets the objective, after which he incorporates it into the project letter and assembles the team. During the first team meeting, the sponsor explains why he is giving the team this particular assignment.

Once the parties have agreed on the project letter, the sponsor leaves the meeting and the kaizen team can begin its analysis.

3. Using the various analysis tools, the team investigates the current state: How is the current process progressing and what are the root causes of the wastes and problems?
4. Once the main root causes have been identified, it is possible to come up with solutions for a new process to be developed: the future state.
5. The final step is to draft an action plan for how the future state and the related solutions will be implemented.

At the end of the Planning phase, the team will present the solutions and the action plan to the sponsor. If the sponsor approves these, it is time to start implementing the plans—i.e., the Do phase.

Do phase—The kaizen team performs all the actions included in the action plan (or has them performed). The team members are responsible for monitoring the progress and quality of the implementation and take action when anything differs from the original objective.

Check phase—During this phase, the team checks the impact of the improvements that have been implemented, comparing the results of the test to the objective set in the project letter and making adjustments during the Act phase, if necessary.

Act phase—The art of improvement is to ensure that things actually do get better and *remain* better. For this purpose, standardization methods are created as part of step 8 (Figure 7.1) in order to embed the improvements in the organization. The team ensures that all parties involved familiarize themselves with the new standards before implementing them.

Below is a detailed overview of the eight steps that make up the cycle of improvement.

Step 1: Choose a Subject

Practice

The Social Services Department of a municipality has a traditional organization that focuses primarily on distributing welfare. The department's new director has noted that the consultants are involved mainly in dealing with these welfare payments, whereas he would like them to focus more on encouraging clients to find

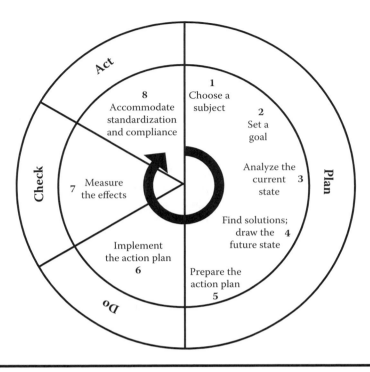

Figure 7.1   The improvement cycle

employment or at least become more socially active. Paradoxically, however, lead time for welfare applications is extremely long. The current director is the third person to hold this position in a short period of time.

This has had an impact on employees. They are tired of the many changes that have been implemented and are reluctant to accept any further change. This is partly because the previous directors had fairly traditional management styles. The new director, however, has innovative ideas about how the welfare application process can be improved in such a way that lead time is significantly reduced and consultants spend less time on each application. However, feeling that his ideas will meet with resistance, he decides it will be more effective to let his employees resolve the problem themselves, and he decides to form kaizen teams. The director acts as the sponsor and states at the beginning of each first kaizen meeting why he feels it is important that the lead time of the process be reduced and why he intends to use a kaizen team to achieve this objective. The reasoning behind this decision is that this will give consultants more time to ensure that people find jobs (Figure 7.2).

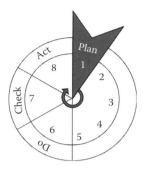

Figure 7.2

During the first meeting, the sponsor explains why this subject was chosen and why it is important that the problem is tackled. This is when the link with the organization's vision is established; for example, the sponsor can explain what will happen with the additional time created if the team is successful. It is important that the team sees that there are no hidden goals, such as a reduction in force (RIF).

The following are typical assignments completed by kaizen teams:

■ Reducing the lead time of work processes, such as granting licenses and grants
■ Reducing the time required to process objections and appeals
■ Reducing the number of complaints
■ Reducing the number of errors made when processing all types of applications
■ Reducing the administrative burden for volunteers
■ Reducing waiting times at counters
■ Improving the quality and efficiency of management processes, such as the planning and control cycle
■ Reducing the number of errors in all types of registrations
■ Improving the performance of chain processes

It is for the sponsor to consider if the subject under debate will improve effectiveness toward the clients. That is to say, will the client notice the positive effects? Although efficiency assignments can lead to cost savings, they may have a negative effect on the organization's effectiveness. It is possible to strike a good balance between effectiveness and efficiency by making the subject about effectiveness in client services and to require that the current efficiency be maintained or improved.

The subjects handled by the kaizen teams are cross-departmental or represent chain processes where participants from the chain participate in the kaizen team. Individuals and representatives from the corporate sector also can be invited to participate. This ensures a variety of creative and exciting combinations—exciting because it offers people the opportunity to look behind the scenes of a public agency.

Public service providers perform both creative tasks and transactional tasks. The majority of tasks are transactional: agreements are signed and processed by the administrative staff. Creative tasks include the development of new services and the establishment of creative partnerships with individuals and corporations. A sponsor may have the vision to reduce the time spent on transactional duties, creating scope for more creative activities. A social services department, for example, can reduce the time spent on transactional duties (e.g., welfare applications, changes, and terminations), thus creating an opportunity to establish, say, a work center (based on the work-first principles) together with a group of people where a variety of creative resources are used to ensure that people get back into the workforce.

Lead Time of a Kaizen Team

To a large extent the choice of subject determines the lead time of a kaizen team. As a general rule, the more limited or simple the subject, the shorter the lead time. The risk involved in a comprehensive or complex subject is that the time the team works on the subject can be very long and, alternatively, the team may lose its overview of the situation or its courage. Experience has shown that the cycle of improvement can sometimes be completed within a single week and need not last longer than several months, including the implementation and embedding of the new process. It becomes easier to divide complex, comprehensive subjects across multiple teams.

When a kaizen team is set up for a subject for which most of the information is readily available, it is possible to make a quick analysis. In reducing lead times, effective time recording and possibly a video of the current situation provide enough information for the assessment and root cause analysis of step 3 in Figure 7.1. In these types of situations, all-day meetings are highly effective. The team members are relieved of their duties for two or three consecutive days in order to complete the first five steps in this cycle of improvement. This cycle culminates in an action plan, and some steps in the action plan may already have been completed. Due to its compactness, this model—the kaizen event—has a major impact on the organization. Although this model is highly effective, it cannot always be implemented, as specific data is lacking for effective analysis. This makes it necessary to first spend time on testing. It also may be practically impossible to relieve employees from their duties for this extended period of time.

Another model is one where the team gathers together for an afternoon once a week. One meeting lasts between two to three hours. You should try to at least keep the time between the meetings limited. If the intervals between the meetings are longer, there is a chance that the background to a particular decision is no longer clear and that it will be necessary to hold the discussion again.

Step 2: Set a Goal

Practice

> *The sponsor's team is not used to working with goals—they believe the effort they put in is more important than the result. In order to build an effective team anyway, the director sets a SMART objective in the project letter, which is based on his knowledge of the lead times of similar processes at other Social Services Departments, plus a large dose of ambition: "to reduce the current average lead time of the application for welfare benefits (i.e., living expenses) to a maximum of 50% of current lead time, realized within one month of the start of the team."*
>
> *The team initially regards the objective as not very realistic, but after an exercise in the form of a game involving the "Eight Deadly Wastes," they feel more comfortable with the objective, and the project letter is approved. The team is now ready to work (Figure 7.3).*

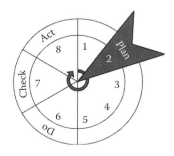

Figure 7.3   Set a goal

In the project letter, the sponsor set a clear goal. However, when is an objective formulated clearly, and what is the value of an objective?

SMART Goals

A well-formulated objective ensures that all parties are aware what the task at hand involves, what needs to be accomplished, and when. In other words, it guides the team in the work they perform. When there is a clear objective, the team will know when they have completed the assignment. Finally, a clear objective motivates the team members to actually achieve the success and offers it the opportunity to celebrate its success. Valuable, well-formulated objectives meet the SMART criteria (**S**pecific, **M**easurable, **A**chievable, **R**ealistic, and **T**ime-based). It is important to make sure that the objective is in line with expectations of the stakeholders in the process, such as members of the public. If the SMART criteria are applied too strictly, especially when combined with a large set of requirements, this also can undermine creativity. Make sure you do not underestimate your team members; they will soon be able to identify the solution even when working with a number of prerequisites. Allow enough scope in the requirements, and make sure the objective is inspiring.

At the start of the kaizen team's first meeting, the sponsor explains the project letter. Point by point, the team goes over the terms of reference, objectives, and prerequisites, with possibly a separate negotiation on the prerequisites. Once there is agreement on the project letter, the team can begin the analysis.

Checklist for steps 1 and 2:

- ☑ The assignment (i.e., the problem) is quantifiable
- ☑ The subject is regarded as a problem by the team members, or they benefit directly from resolving the problem
- ☑ The objective is based on SMART
- ☑ The objective is inspiring and has a clear link to what people perceive as "value"
- ☑ The prerequisites listed in the project letter are clear and nonrestrictive
- ☑ The sponsor guarantees time and financial resources for the team
- ☑ Middle management/the management team supports the approach by setting up a kaizen team and warrants that employees will be relieved temporarily from their duties

☑ Middle management/the management team agrees to the fact that solutions that meet the prerequisites will be implemented

☑ The project letter was prepared by the sponsor (and not by the kaizen leader)

☑ The sponsor discussed the project letter with the kaizen team

Step 3: Analyze the Current State

Practice

The leader of the kaizen team wants to start analyzing the process but is soon presented with a wide variety of solutions. The team really wants to proceed to step 4: "Finding solutions." There is a risk that only obvious solutions are mentioned and that these result from a lack of knowledge of the current process. The team leader manages to direct the discussion toward the subject of assessment by asking that the current process be identified first. The first step is the process analysis (Figure 7.4).

People tend to think in terms of solutions, and it is likely that solutions will be presented at the initial meeting. However, there is a risk that these solutions will not be effective, as there is not yet a common and comprehensive assessment of the current situation. Step 3 outlines the team's common vision of the question: How does the current process really work?

At the start of the analysis, the impression of how the current process works may vary for each team member. From their own position in the process, they often lack a comprehensive overview of the process as a whole, which can sometimes result in ineffective discussions. In order to prevent this, team members together describe the current situation in detail, using drawings,

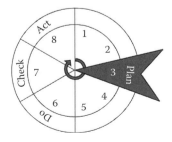

Figure 7.4 Analyze the current state

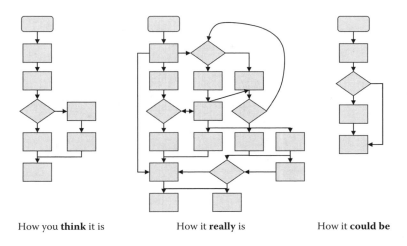

How you **think** it is How it **really** is How it **could be**

Figure 7.5

photos, and manuals. You should never assume that everyone knows how the entire process works in detail, as this is usually not the case. As long as individual members of the team have different ideas about a specific situation, they will be unable to present a shared opinion and make sound decisions. In some cases, each individual employee will have his or her own way of working in the process, with each team member judging a situation based on his or her own impression of the situation. And, as long as ideas about the current situation differ, so will opinions about the best solutions.

The team does not base its impression of how the current process works on a process description someone retrieved from the quality system, as this is often obsolete or relates to theory rather than the actual situation (Figure 7.5). In order to gain an accurate impression of the current situation, it is essential to identify the actual situation using the value stream map (VSM) included in Chapter 4, which means a detailed process description of the real process, including all kinds of semi-illegal bypasses rather than the descriptions from the quality manuals. Based on a common assessment of the current situation, it is possible to identify the causes as to why, for example, lead time is currently so long or why the process is so prone to error.

Practice

> *The kaizen team outlines the current process using a VSM. The next step is to identify bottlenecks in the process using different-colored Post-its®. The team starts to get excited; the team members all start*

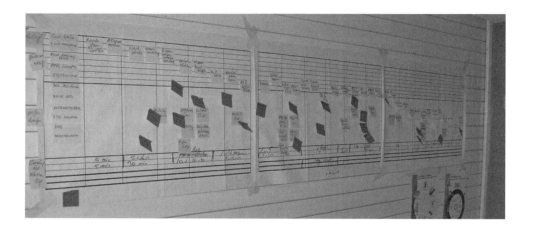

Figure 7.6 Current state map

*yelling, and the noise level rises. The team leader then intervenes
and makes sure that each member of the team is given the opportunity to speak. Because he does not know much about the actual
subject, he is in a good position to supervise the group process.
Is everyone getting a chance to speak and are the team members
listening to each other? During the process of charting the current
process, team members are asked about action times and lead times
for each step of the process. Note that the times listed are intuitive
and the team leader decides that these times must be verified in
practice. At the end of the day, the participants are given the assignment to collect these times and add them to the Current State map.
Figure 7.6 shows a photo of the Current State map produced by this
kaizen team.*

Process Analysis: Looking for the Hidden Process

Before outlining the current situation, it is important to first answer the
questions of what products and services result from the process, who
the client is (i.e., what role does a member of the public have here?), and
what their explicit and implicit needs and requirements are. Based on this
information, it can then be determined which activities add value and what
the wastes will be.

Next, the current situation is identified in as much detail as possible—the
more detailed the outline, the more visible the wastes will be. Each step
of the process is identified and analyzed, and, for each act, team members

answer the questions: Why are we doing this? and Why are we doing it like this? The analysis then identifies the value-creating actions and shows where the deadly wastes are concentrated.

For the current situation, you will find answers to such questions as:

- How many "products" do we create in each period?
- What are the minimum and maximum lead times?
- What is the action time per action?
- Is the sequence of activities logical?
- How many transfers occur (the more handovers, the longer the lead time)?
- Where are the intermediary stocks (WIP), and how large are they?
- How many checks are performed and why? Specify the checks.
- Is each step in the process necessary?
- Are there multiple routes?
- Are different working methods used that lead to the same (or a better) result?
- Where and how often is data stored?
- Can we find all required information and materials within 30 seconds?
- What checks are performed, and why are they performed?

From Initial Assessment to Root Causes

Eliminating wastes and resolving errors is possible only when we know why they were caused in the first place. A 5 × Why diagram can be a key tool in identifying root causes (see Appendix C). In this diagram, the causes that resulted from the brainstorming session are placed in the upper row behind the word "problem." The first question is: Why do we have the problem?" For each cause, the "Why" question is asked again. This method is called 5 × Why. This does not necessarily mean that you must always ask the question five times, but you must ask it at least until there are no sensible answers left. The figure in the appendix shows an elaboration of one of the causes resulting from a brainstorming session—in this case, the question "Why" was asked five times. In the example, the fourth "Why" question is: "Why are C-forms not prioritized?" The answer is: "Because there is no instruction to do so." The fifth question, then, might be: "Why is there no instruction?" The answer to this question is no longer relevant ("Because there isn't."). A root cause has been identified and a potential solution is available.

Checklist for step 3:

- ☑ It has been demonstrated that the subject selected truly constitutes a problem
- ☑ A comprehensive assessment has been made of the current state
- ☑ The root causes of the wastes have been identified
- ☑ All team members agree on the choice of the main causes
- ☑ Where necessary, the root causes have been checked for accuracy
- ☑ The current state has been discussed with the sponsor

Step 4: Find Solutions, Draw the Future State

Practice

Before the kaizen leader assigns his team to reflect on the future situation, he asks that the ideal situation be outlined from the perspective of a client. The team members can't really get the debate going and have a hard time putting themselves in the client's shoes. However, after some time, a situation is outlined that is ideal to the clients. Next, the leader asks the team members to outline the ideal situation from the perspective of the community at large.

Based on these two conceptual models, the team is encouraged to look beyond the obvious solutions. The team starts by outlining the Future State, which can be achieved within the period specified in the project letter (Figure 7.7).

Based on the analysis described in step 3, the team creates solutions that will help ensure that the objective is achieved. Such solutions may involve

Figure 7.7   Find solutions, etc.

methods to prevent errors or even an all new work process, including all the measures that need to be taken to achieve them.

Possible Solutions

There are a number of points that can be used as a guideline when conceiving a new and improved process:

Collecting Data

During processes, you should collect as little data as possible and generate as much information as possible. *Note*: Information and data are not the same thing. Data essentially has no value unless it can be converted into usable information. The telephone directory, for example, is filled with address details and telephone numbers, and among all those hundreds of thousands of data, there is that one telephone number (i.e., the information) that you need. The objective, therefore, is not to collect data, but to create information. There are three reasons that justify data collection:

1. The relevant data is converted into information that allows the processes to run more smoothly.
2. The relevant data is collected and converted into information because this meets a public need.
3. The relevant data is collected and converted into information because this is required by law.

The process of collecting data that will not be converted into information, or that *is* converted into information but not for any of the purposes listed above, serves no purpose and should be discontinued.

Work on the Basis of the 'One is Best' Principle

Check whether acts are performed more than once in the process. Next, find methods to ensure that acts need only be performed once: one phone call, one visit from the client, one decision, one signature, one result, one sheet of paper, one contact person, etc. The motto of one particular municipality in Great Britain is: "One call, one visit, one decision—one result." Other forms of these "one is best" method include: using one-page memos, attending one-hour meetings, and making one-day decisions (i.e., decisions that are made within a single day.)

Investigate All Checks in the Organization

For each check or double check in a process, it is good to establish why it is performed. If it is a statutory requirement, you should demonstrate this by citing the relevant provisions. Sometimes, the check in question may have become redundant following a change in legislation or due to an inaccurate interpretation, while the check is, in fact, still in place. In other cases, a particular check may have been introduced over 30 years ago following a controversial incident. And, even though that incident has never been repeated, the entire system is still extremely secure.

File Only Once—in Only One Place

Coworkers who share an office and attend the same meetings receive the same meeting reports. All of these reports are printed out and stored in personal files, and the same space is used to file the same report, only in a different place.

Process Ownership

In task-oriented organizations, someone is responsible for a set of tasks, but no one is responsible for the process as a whole. As a result, all employees perform their work adequately and check for any deviations, but at the same time no one manages the comprehensive process. In process improvement processes, you must make sure that there is a process owner who is responsible for ensuring that the process runs effectively and efficiently, even if, or especially if, the process is cross-departmental.

Eliminate the Need for Checks

Checks are one of the eight deadly wastes. In addition to eliminating double checks, approvals, and signatures, you must consider whether checks are necessary at all. If things go well all the time, there is no longer any need for checks, but also not if the result of error is acceptable. Processes include checks to correct errors; as soon as the word "error" is mentioned, you set out to identify the causes. An important reason why people make errors is a lack of knowledge, and training employees can prevent errors and eliminate the need for checks. And, if you do feel there should be a check or if this is required by law, find out if a coworker, rather than a manager, can perform the check.

Create the Process Based on Averages

In designing the new work processes, there is a strong tendency to outline a process based on an extremely difficult application that was filed on one occasion. This means that all kinds of additional steps (such as checks) that are required for that external case also apply to all other applications by default. Therefore, you should establish the process based on averages, or distinguish between a bulk process for "easy" cases and a separate process for complex cases.

Get the Job Done as Soon as You Start Work

In some cases, it may be efficient to collect work until you have an entire batch and only then start handling it. You could, for example, process all applications in a single afternoon. From the perspective of the client, this method is not effective, as it creates additional waiting time. It is important to structure the process in such a way that any questions received are answered immediately; there will no longer be a collection of applications, and lead time is minimal.

Duty to Report Rather Than the Requirement to Hold a Permit

Processing a permit application is time-consuming, and an alternative would be to just report specific events or incidents to the authorities. For example, neighborhood residents are not required to apply for a permit to organize a block party, but they *are* required to report it to the municipal counter. The applicant is then given a "block party package" containing items with which to block off and maybe deck out the street. This leads to substantial cost savings (i.e., it is efficient) and reduces lead time significantly.

Completing Transactions from Home

If you intend to visit one of the more popular museums but don't want to stand in line, you can purchase tickets online and print them out yourself. Once you have the tickets, you don't need to line up at the ticket desk, but can walk straight through. This would be the ideal situation for people required to apply for a permit: You answer a series of questions on your computer screen, and once the system has approved your application, you can print out the permit.

Look Around You

Ideas for improvement may originate in your own sector, but it is also possible to borrow ideas from other sectors. These solutions may not always be obvious, and yet they could be revolutionary. Assertive parents of children with special needs who live in a secure environment with other children want what is best for their child, which means that they will ensure that any agreements made regarding the number of hours of supervision and support for their children are honored. This involves an additional burden for the staff, as they are required each time to publish detailed reports on the activities they performed with the client. A smart system from another sector: There are restaurants where the waiters take your order using a small palmtop computer, which instantly transmits the orders to the bar and kitchen. If healthcare workers were to use the same system, they would no longer need desktop computers to prepare reports. In addition, it would significantly reduce the chances of an employee forgetting a reservation or an appointment.

Letting a Certified Architect Assess the Building Permit

Rather than having the municipal authority assess applications for building permits, a certified architect would assess the permits.

Handle Reports and Complaints by Making a Phone Call

Processing for handling complaints and objections requires a great deal of time and paper, and experience has shown that people don't usually need the process that they generate as a result of filing an objection or complaint. In fact, the majority of complaints and objections are not really that at all. People normally file these objections and complaints to ask the government for a clarification after it has failed to provide clear information. When these people receive a phone call from a civil servant and are given the opportunity to ask their question, any ambiguities and misunderstandings are cleared up and the person withdraws his/her complaint or report.

Remove the Member of the Public from the Process

In many countries, individuals annually spend hours filing their tax returns. In many cases, the revenue service already has this data in its possession or would be able to obtain it from other government agencies. In the majority of countries, employers are required to provide the revenue service with details on their employees' pay. In other countries, people no longer need to file their tax returns because the revenue service has enough information on people to be able to calculate and compile the tax return itself. Although you might think many people will object to this, the fact is that most of them are pretty happy with the system as it is.

Ensure Smooth Front Office Processes

The reason why processes are so complex is often the result of front-end processes. People are not always sure how to complete forms and what impact the incorrect completion of such a form will have on the rest of the process. Farther down the process, this will then lead to ambiguities and misunderstandings. Providing clear input ensures a smoother process. Make sure that the front office is effective enough in helping people fill out their applications as clearly as possible.

Establishing Specialized Workplaces

People have fixed workplaces and take on the work that they are expected to perform. An alternative is to establish a fixed workplace for a dedicated task only, which the employee uses whenever there is this task to be done. A section of the office is designed and standardized in such a way that the employee can handle everything as soon as he or she enters the office. The result is that the workplace no longer needs to be changed when the employee needs to perform a different kind of job. Instead, he or she simply walks to another workplace, where yet another type of work is performed. This saves a lot of time looking for and storing or filing particular items.

The Ideal Situation

Many of these ideas for improvement are less than obvious, and to ensure that team members will think beyond the most obvious solutions, it is recommended to have them outline the ideal situation at the start of step 4. This is the ideal situation from the perspective of the individuals (in their role as citizens), which is based on the assumption that there are no practical barriers. These brainstorming sessions often lead to ideas that may initially seem a little unorthodox, but that, once they have been adapted, can easily be implemented in employees' own situations. These are innovative improvements that currently are not used anywhere in the public sector.

IT as a Solution

IT workers are "fundamentalists" in fact they believe that software always provides the solution. Digitization is an obvious choice when improving work processes and reducing lead times; digitizing processes or workflow can be regarded as a form of standardization. If a process has an illogical structure, you can digitize it and win time in the process. However, at that point, the process has not been made logical yet, has not yet been adapted to the needs of the public, and the deadly wastes have not yet been eliminated. There is particular cause for concern when the work processes are adapted to the software. Some service providers are perfectly digitized at the front end, offering a digital counter with the opportunity to file all kinds of applications through the Web site. However, this digital façade can sometimes conceal a traditional organization with work processes that are rife with deadly wastes.

If work processes are redesigned logically and effectively, it is worth assessing whether analog would not be just as effective, and even if it's not perfect, it's always possible to do a little tweaking. Once the optimal situation has been reached, you need to consider whether the process can be automated and, if so, if that will actually improve it. Digitization is not discussed until step 8 of the cycle of improvement, "Standardization and Compliance."

Automation may have advantages over a paper system, in that digital information is usually more up-to-date than printed information. With digitized systems, double data entry is no longer necessary, and the input of required information can be guaranteed by adding required fields. However, it is the processes, rather than the software, that form the basis, as technology should always play a subservient role.

Temporary Solutions

Solutions conceived by the team have the status of potential solutions. Once solutions have been conceived, they are not implemented immediately, but first are developed into specific proposals for improvement (Appendix D).

The solutions were created based on the knowledge and experience of the team members and must produce the desired effect without any adverse side effects. In order to be more certain of the impact of the solution, the team can prepare a hypothesis in which it carefully sets out its expectations of the impact of the solution and tests it in practice or in a simulation. Enter the solutions only after the analysis is completed and the comprehensive future state has been presented to the sponsor.

Risk Analysis

There is also a danger inherent in modifications made to current systems and processes. Specifically, a modification may lead to an improvement in one process while causing a relapse in another. Alternatively, there may be an unacceptably high risk related to errors or illegal acts. It is up to the kaizen teams to identify the risks and determine whether measures are necessary. Solutions also can be changed based on this analysis, or can be cancelled altogether.

Checklist for step 4:

- ☑ All solutions have been incorporated into the future state
- ☑ A cost-benefit analysis has been made
- ☑ The risks of adverse side effects have been identified and discussed
- ☑ If possible, the team has tested whether the solutions actually work
- ☑ The solutions have been assessed against the requirements

Step 5: Prepare the Action Plan

Practice

> *The kaizen team has outlined a new process by which lead time has been significantly reduced and action time for the consultants has been reduced by more than 50%. A number of actions must be*

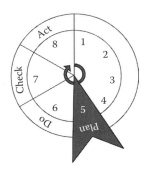

Figure 7.8   Prepare the action plan

performed to move from the old to the new situations; these actions are assessed and recorded in an action plan. The sponsor, along with the management team, was invited to attend a presentation about the progress made so far. The presentation ends with a brief discussion on the future state and the action plan. The sponsor approves the implementation of the action plan; he says that he will ensure that there is sufficient support from the management (Figure 7.8).

The action plan is a schedule of all actions that will ensure that the solutions can be implemented. It specifies who is responsible for what action point, whether financial resources or equipment are required, and when the process should be completed. Technical changes to be implemented by third parties, such as changes to existing software, require a detailed description—an outline of the desired situation can help in this process.

The Sponsor

Before the action plan is implemented, there is a moment at which the team presents the future state and the action plan to the sponsor. At that moment, the team can gain formal approval from the sponsor to implement the action plan. In the interim presentation (Figure 7.9), the sponsor can assess whether the team can properly substantiate the future state and whether all action points comply with the requirements listed in the project letter (Appendix B).

Although this may sound simple, it can potentially be difficult for a sponsor. What if the solutions presented are perfectly in line with the requirements, but the sponsor himself has, in his opinion, better solutions? Or what if the sponsor doesn't believe that the solutions presented are appropriate and is

Figure 7.9 Kaizen presentation

certain that they won't be effective? If, as a sponsor, you decide to speak up and not accept the solutions presented, you effectively take over the assignment from the team. The ownership is gone, and both team members and the sponsor are disappointed. On the other hand, it hurts to see the team implementing an action plan of which you know (or think you know) that it won't lead to anything. Experience has shown that sponsors tend to think that without any reason. If a team does not come up with the same ideas as those you have conceived as a sponsor, this does not mean that their ideas are not good. In fact, they may even be better.

The team members may show a reverse reaction. If the sponsor, upon presenting the project letter, says that he will accept all solutions that comply with the requirements, the team members might look at him somewhat incredulously. It's the first time they have ever seen a manager who does not veto an idea for improvement at the last minute or want to change it to suit his taste. Seeing is believing. It is important to be very consistent as a sponsor:

I will accept solutions that comply with the requirements.

Just wait and see—ideas are often smarter than you think, and they actually *work*. As a sponsor, you exercise control over the quality of the solutions through the requirements listed in the project letter and by assembling an effective team. As a sponsor, try to let go and accept everything that meets the requirements, even if it goes against your instincts.

Informing Coworkers

During the improvement process, you may encounter resistance from managers or colleagues. Kaizen teams often have to go against the grain, and to avoid this as much as possible, it is important to involve everyone in the assignment and solutions at an early stage. For example, the sponsor might draft the project letter together with his management team. The progress of the kaizen team is communicated through periodic bulletins or information boards as well as through regular work meetings. It is recommended that, at the time the outlines of solutions are becoming clear, team members discuss this with their coworkers. In addition to increasing support, this prevents team tunnel vision; everything they think of is good. As a result, they may lack the essential critical attitude and healthy sense of reality.

Full transparency of the improvements conceived is vital. Coworkers who are not part of the kaizen team enjoy hearing and seeing what the team is doing; however, they are primarily interested in the solutions, as this will affect their work as well. Open communication will reduce the chances of resistance to the solutions. Everyone must be given the opportunity to respond to the kaizen team's proposals, but make sure to explain that the team ultimately decides which solutions will be implemented. After all, they are the ones who were given the assignment.

Checklist for step 5:

- ☑ The future state and the action plan have been presented to the sponsor
- ☑ All proposals for improvement have been discussed with the coworkers
- ☑ In this presentation, the team explained how the analysis resulted in the solutions
- ☑ There is clarity regarding the required resources and support in implementing the action plan

Step 6: Implement the Action Plan

Practice

Large sheets of paper detailing the future state are hanging on the wall near the coffee machine. There has been much discussion about the team's progress, and now it is crunch time. The members of the kaizen team have been working in the Department of Social Services long enough to know that many projects get bogged down during the implementation stage. However, the sponsor is eager for the project to be completed successfully and within the time frame set. Together with the team leader, he ensures that the assignment the team is working on is prioritized, so that there is enough focus on implementing the proposals for improvement in the organization. The team leader ensures that he remains up-to-date on the progress made on all action points (Figure 7.10).

Once the action plan and the proposals for improvement have been approved, they can be implemented. The team members perform a number of actions themselves or pass the work on to specialists in the organization. The kaizen team remains responsible for coordination; they check whether the actions are implemented correctly and whether everything is working according to expectation, intervening when necessary. It is vitally important that the required changes of software or documents are described in detail in the proposals for improvement (Appendix D). The team members inform the team leader about the progress of the actions; the team leader follows the schedule and makes adjustments if necessary. In addition, he provides a comprehensive overview of the progress of the actions and reports this to the team leaders and the sponsor.

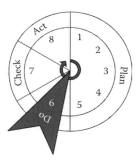

Figure 7.10   Implement the action plan

Checklist for step 6:

☑ Continually check whether the schedule included in the action plan is implemented

☑ Check whether the actions are implemented as intended

Step 7: Measure the Effects

Practice

> *The team gathers together to discuss the progress. Some action points have already been implemented; the team is now waiting for the IT department, which has promised to make some minor changes to the existing software. It has been agreed that an implemented action point is only completed when the kaizen team is satisfied. There are no comments about the quality of the implementation; everything is going according to plan (Figure 7.11).*
>
> *Lead time has been measured throughout the entire improvement process. Lead time has been reduced by more than 50%, and it appears that the team will achieve its objectives.*

The team meanwhile has implemented all the solutions and the new process is effective. Naturally, they expect that the total contribution of all solutions has ensured that the objective has been met. The team checks whether this is the case by continuously measuring the results, using the same test as when measuring the objective.

Results with Kaizen Teams

The results achieved by kaizen teams can be spectacular, even though the solutions are amazingly simple.

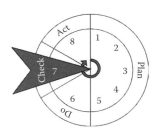

Figure 7.11   Measure the effects

Several practical results:

- A 50% reduction in lead time in processing complaints (municipal governments)
- A 30 to 75% reduction in action time in granting specific licenses
- A 60% reduction in lead time in the process of applying for financial support
- A 90% reduction in administrative errors (municipal governments)
- A 75% reduction in filing space (government departments)
- Reducing the process of handling complaints from more than three months to less than five days

(For more information, see Chapter 9.)

What If the Objective Is Not Met?

If the results do not meet the objective, it can be disappointing to both the team and the sponsor. What is important now is that the team not give up. If they do, it is up to the team leader to get the process back on track.

The team then completes the cycle again, but the other way around. Do not address the issue right away, but start out by analyzing step 6, the implementation of the action plan. Have the actions been implemented correctly? If so, analyze step 5, etc.

Checklist for step 7:

☑ Is measured the same way as in the process of determining the objective (step 2)

☑ How do the results of the measurement relate to the objective set?

☑ If the results are disappointing, you must complete the cycle from back to front in order to analyze why

Step 8: Accommodate Standardization and Compliance

Practice

During the analysis phase and while implementing the action points, the team members received some feedback from coworkers. This feedback was positive, although there were also some critical points,

Figure 7.12   Accommodate standardization and compliance

most of which were related to the proposals for improvement. Several coworkers would have handled certain issues differently, and the team focused on this aspect. The points raised by coworkers were all addressed by the team, and those who raised the points received feedback. However, not everyone can be satisfied (Figure 7.12).

Throughout the project, the sponsor emphasized that the new process should be simpler than the previous one in order to encourage the employees to start using the new method.

The new process has already been tested and has turned out to be successful. Several minor points still need to be worked out. However, not all employees work according to this new method, and the purpose of the eighth and final step in the cycle of improvement is to establish a standard (i.e., standardization) and ensuring that everyone works according to this standard (i.e., compliance).

The kaizen team is responsible for designing effective standards that ensure compliance. The improved process can always be improved further. Once it has been in place for a year, if the same or a different team were to reevaluate it, this could lead to an even better version of the process. Make sure you don't cast the administrative process in stone, making it virtually impossible to implement any improvements in the future. The more time a process is given to mature, the more the process participants will be convinced that things really can't get any better.

(For more information on standardization and compliance, see Chapter 8.)

Ensuring Sustainability through Performance Indicators

Kaizen teams tend to fear that the result will fade once the team has been dissolved. The issue has received a lot of attention because of all the focus on the team; they are focused on performing as well as possible. When the team is dissolved, the solutions are transferred to the line organization, which is subsequently responsible for ensuring compliance. The kaizen team has ensured a simple method that can easily be taught and transferred. The team's objective can be maintained as a performance indicator in order to ensure that the team remains focused. In the practical example, the results are continuously measured and reported, as well as being discussed during the weekly meeting of the department and the management team. This ensures that the results remain in focus and that it is possible to intervene if necessary.

Completion

As soon as the solutions have been transferred to the standing organization and all employees are working in accordance with the new procedures, the team is dissolved. As soon as the results have been embedded in the organization, the kaizen team can officially end the cycle of improvement with a final presentation. In addition to presenting for the sponsor, they also include coworkers and managers of other departments. The final presentation details the team's achievements and explains how these achievements were made possible. It is recommended to structure the presentation based on the eight steps in the cycle of improvement. For each step, the result then can be presented. The intention is to encourage the support of those present for the team's performance during the final presentation. All team members should preferably participate in the presentation, making it clear that it is a team performance.

The team has successfully completed the assignment and achieved the result. This success must be celebrated, as celebrating success is important in recognizing the team's performance, as well as a token of appreciation for the flexibility and creativity demonstrated by the team members. A fun, playful reward may be a good way to honor the team's work. A bonus is not such a good idea, as this sends out the message that ideas for improvement will be rewarded financially. It is better to come up with something creative and original, something that people will remember for a long time to come.

Checklist for step 8:

☑ A compliance plan is in place

☑ The Compliance Pyramid in Chapter 8 was used to select the compliance measures

☑ The team has ensured that all parties involved are informed and have been trained in the new procedures

☑ It is checked whether the new procedures are actually used

☑ Has the final presentation been given?

☑ Has it been communicated within the organization that the team has been dissolved?

☑ Have the successes been celebrated?

Chapter 8

Standardization and Compliance

Compliance

Recording the procedures to be followed in a standard is one thing; ensuring that they are complied with at all times is another, and it's at least as important. Standardization and compliance are inextricably linked, and a standard that contains no provisions for compliance will have no effect at all. We have all seen the folders with procedures and operating instructions on the shelves of the quality department, which no one ever consults. The choice of the form used for the working agreement depends on the level to which this agreement must be complied with. If a departure from the standard can result in a fatal accident, it is essential to ensure full compliance, thereby simply eliminating unsafe alternatives. There are other factors at play as well, such as the level of flexibility employees show in complying with standards.

Many regard standards as overly restrictive, as they require that people abandon their own alternatives and comply with another method. However, proper standards are set by joint agreement, and the objective should be to integrate employees' best practices into a single, common standard. By always performing activities in the same tried-and-tested order, it is possible to prevent waiting times, errors, and disruptions, which is sure to benefit all employees. Once you no longer need to consider every single action because an effective standard is in place, it is possible to focus on other, more interesting activities, such as analyzing errors, processing complex applications, and devising process improvement solutions.

Conscious and Subconscious Actions

Scientific study has shown that at least 95% of our actions are subconscious and automatic, which is to say that we often operate on automatic pilot. When you are driving, you don't constantly think about what foot you should use on what pedal. This applies not only to driving, but also to checking your e-mail, conducting meetings, entering data, and all types of everyday tasks. Research has demonstrated that the activities you perform at least once a week eventually enter into your subconscious mind; you don't even have to give them a second thought. That's a good thing, as it enables us to multitask—e.g., type an e-mail to a friend while talking on the phone. However, there are disadvantages as well. Once a particular procedure has been embedded in our mind, it is difficult to change it. Although you might try to make people aware of the risk or inconvenience of performing tasks automatically by suggesting improvements, chances are they will soon revert to their own routines despite your best efforts. Even if you persuasively argue the merits of a new set of procedures, this may not always convince people to break their old habits.

One way of making sure a new standard is absorbed is to instruct everyone and monitor their compliance for months, taking immediate action as soon as anyone deviates. Over time, all employees will have been conditioned and their behavior will have become automatic. However, this is the complicated way of doing things. This chapter addresses other alternatives for changing people's behavior by using standards.

Why Operating Instructions and Procedures Don't Always Work

The word *standardization* is associated with procedures and operating instructions. People tend to have a great deal of faith in written agreements, assuming that something will be effective just because it is written down. However, written standards only appear to provide security; in fact, the least effective forms of compliance are in text form, such as procedures and instructions. It is extremely likely that they will not be read, let alone remembered; and, in addition, it is complex and time-consuming to keep everything updated, both in the manuals and in the minds of all parties involved. A general rule is that the longer the text, the smaller the chance that people actually will read it. The majority of people will readily admit that they have never read or barely read the instruction manual to their DVD player, or even their car manual. Text is at the most scanned for images or words that attract attention. People usually give it the old college try. If it turns out that a particular method works, we just remember what we did to get it right. Even if someone has read the procedures, there is no guarantee that they will actually comply with them.

On top of that, the more procedures and instructions there are, the more compliance monitoring is involved, the larger the amount of paperwork, and the more time is required to ensure it is all up to date. It's important to ensure that new and improved procedures are easier to implement than the old alternatives. If this proves impossible, you should try to eliminate any unwanted alternatives.

There are far more effective compliance measures to be conceived than just written instructions, and the next paragraph sets out the four levels of compliance measures based on the Compliance Pyramid.

The Compliance Pyramid

Standardization is useful to you, but even more so to others. When establishing a standard, it's important to consider whose behavior you would like to influence and in what situation. If you are to set a standard for employees who will use it when working the counter (client interactions often take no more than several minutes), you should find a form of standardization that is immediately available to users and whose purpose is immediately clear.

Ideal standards:

■ Contain little or no text at all, but are created using photos and other images, as these attract attention.
■ Immediately communicate the purpose, without the need for interpretation.
■ Are adapted to the user's world and language, which is why the most effective standards are established by those who will use them.

- Do not first have to be retrieved from a file (i.e., they are immediately available).
- Are maintenance free—i.e., no version management is required.
- Do not contain any language barriers.
- Have no alternatives, as these have been blocked.
- Are more effective, more secure, and faster than any current alternatives available. Users are pleased to exchange their imperfect standards for them.
- Work, even though you don't see them. They subconsciously guide people's conduct in the right direction.

Murphy's law roughly states: "If an incident is frequently repeated and there is a small chance each time that something will go wrong, sooner or later it will go wrong." What he meant to say was that even errors that have a small chance of occurring will occur sooner or later. It is possible to predict the probability of process errors and assess the seriousness of the impact. The combination of error probability and consequential loss will help you determine what compliance measures should be implemented.

It is possible to create an effective standardization method using the Compliance Pyramid (Figure 8.1). Start at the top of the pyramid. Is it possible to come up with a fail-safe? If not, explore the option of using visual control tools, and so on. Note that the weakest form of compliance is the

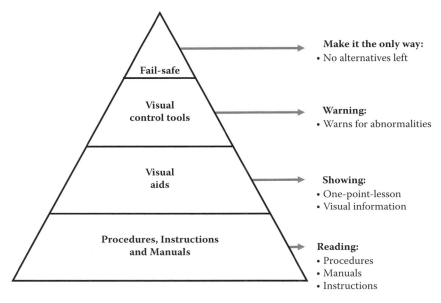

Figure 8.1 The compliance pyramid

procedure or instruction. The lower it is positioned in the pyramid, the less likely there will be compliance and the more monitoring is required to enforce the standard. By corollary, the lower it is positioned on the pyramid, the more time is required to maintain and monitor enforcement.

The Four Levels Explained in Detail

Level 1: The Fail-Safe

Compliance through fail-safes provides the highest level of security. A fail-safe is a compliance method that provides for only one option to do something; this is the most effective option, and any alternatives are blocked. Some condescending managers refer to this form of compliance as "idiot proof."

The possible consequences of the deviations from the standard of course decide what compliance method works most effectively. If a deviation from the standard procedure could result in an accident, a fail-safe is the most appropriate solution. However, even for deviations that would have only minor consequences, a fail-safe may be feasible. In the majority of cases, fail-safes are very simple and economical, as well as highly efficient, so remember to work from the top down in the pyramid.

In administrative process, fail-safes are embedded in the software. This is known as Defensive Design. Examples of fail-safes in administrative processes include:

- Required input fields in software (if you forget to enter the required information, you can't proceed to the next step).
- Instead of numerical fields where any amount can be entered, you create an optional menu containing only several standard amounts.
- The steps completed in administrative software; the system is designed such that the user is automatically directed from one step to the next. This is referred to as "workflow software."

Postcompletion Error

People performing actions of whatever kind focus primarily on the main task. Pumping gas, for example, would classify as a main task, whereas screwing the cap back on would be considered a side task. Withdrawing cash from an ATM is a main task, removing your bank card from the machine is a side task. We tend to forget these side tasks, particularly when they immediately follow the main task. This is a common error also in the workplace (e.g., forgetting to attach a file to an e-mail). The name for this typically human foible is "postcompletion error." Fail-safes can be used to prevent errors in the examples discussed: the gas cap in being replaced by a flap that shuts automatically when the nozzle is removed, so you don't leave it at the station any more. In the example of the ATM, you can collect your cash only after you have removed your card.

Fail-safes are not always feasible and, in some cases, they are too expensive. Lower down the compliance pyramid we discover other forms of standardization.

Level 2: Visual and Audible Control Tools

Visual control tools direct our behavior by sending out signals as soon as there are or will be deviations. These signals may be visual, but noise also can qualify as a control tool. Visual control tools require little or no explanation. It is instantly clear what their purpose is. However, there is no guarantee that there won't be undesirable situations. The impact of these 100% control tools may be lost if there are too many false alarms; in some office buildings, for example, the fire alarm sounds so frequently that everyone remains seated, even when there is a fire.

Examples of visual control tools:

- Passport photos must comply with specific measurements; this is checked by a transparency containing colored frames. This transparency can be placed across the passport photo, making it possible to instantly see whether the measurements are correct.
- Some software applications display error messages when you make an incorrect calculation.
- G-mail contains an option where, if you send an e-mail containing the word "attachment" but forget to actually attach the file, a pop-up appears with a text alert (this feature is known as the "forgotten attachment detector").

Poka Yoke

In the mid-1960s, in order to prevent products with quality deviations from being shipped to customers, it was common to test products using spot checks. The results of the test would then determine whether or not a batch of previously manufactured products had an acceptable error rate and could be shipped to a customer. The Japanese engineer Shigeo Shingo decided there must be ways to detect these quality deviations at an earlier stage or, preferably, to prevent them altogether. He developed poka yoke, which translates roughly as "error-free production." The purpose of poka yoke is to eliminate product deviations by preventing them from occurring or by detecting and correcting them at an early stage. The majority of poka yokes are minor adjustments to the design of a process. There are two types of poka yokes:

1. Prevention poka yokes: Preventing deviations from occurring (e.g., a car can only be started after the driver has put on his seatbelt).
2. Detection poka yokes: Identifying deviations at the earliest possible stage (e.g., a car starts to beep as soon as the driver drives off without a seatbelt).

In the Compliance Pyramid discussed above, a prevention poka yoke is equivalent to a fail-safe, while a detection poka yoke falls into the visual control tools category. Poka yokes have the same features as fail-safes and control tools. They are simple, smart, and cheap. The best area to apply them is close to where deviations might arise. This makes it possible to respond immediately.

A Push in the Right Direction

In addition to being implemented in cases where deviation occurs, control tools can be used to give employees or individuals a push in the right direction. If there are many alternatives, control tools can make sure that the lesser alternatives are not chosen easily. This can be done by hiding unwanted alternatives, or making them unattractive, or by prominently displaying the desired alternative in such a way that it becomes the obvious choice. This is what happens to customers of public service corporations. The corporation prefers direct debit to invoice. They stimulate this by offering a discount if the customer agrees to direct debit. Invoicing is discouraged by no longer offering it as an option to new customers or by only making it possible to revert to invoicing after the customer has agreed to direct debit and after he or she has submitted a written request to have the situation reverted.

Level 3: Visual Aids

A visual aid offers information about processes and standard situations. Visual aids contain little or no text at all. Photos, ideographs, images, and graphics make matters clear faster. Every picture tells a story.

If an operating instruction really is the only way in which the standard can be cast, it should be a visual operating instruction with lots of pictures, cartoon-style. The safety instruction of airliners is based on this principle. This sort of visual operating instruction is called one-point lessons (OPL).

Visual aids are weaker compliance measures than visual control tools because they are less effective in drawing a person's attention to deviating circumstances or potentially dangerous situations. Visual aids also are there when the situation is normal.

Examples of visual aids:

■ Lines and squares on the floor
■ A notice board in the department with outstanding and settled requests
■ Influencing visitors' behavior at the counter of a local government office (from a color scheme on the Web site you can tell what part of the day it's busy and when it's quiet)

Example of better operating instructions: Visual operating instructions (OPL with photos, pictures, and cartoons).

Level 4: Procedures, Instructions, and Manuals

The least effective form of compliance is in text form, such as procedures and instructions. It is extremely likely that they will not be read, let alone be remembered. The more people have to read, the smaller the chance that they will do so. In addition, it is complex and time-consuming to keep everything updated, both in the manuals and in the minds of all parties involved. Ask any employee if he or she can show you a particular work instruction within 30 seconds.

Plus, the fact that people have read the procedures is no guarantee that they will actually comply with them. People often develop their own working method, and, if it's simpler than the official one (even if the official procedure is better), they are very likely to use their own method, and certainly if their personal assessment of possible direct averse effects is small (Figure 8.2).

Make sure that instructions can be found close to where they are needed. For instance, hang up process descriptions (flow charts) in large print in the department that uses them.

Figure 8.2   This photograph symbolizes how people react to standards when they classify them as inconvenient or when they have a better or quicker alternative. This barrier is placed here for safety reasons to prevent bikers from passing. They have to go 30 feet out of their way to pass somewhere else. This standard is not a failsafe. The quick route is left open: Bikers pass the barrier on the right. This illegal path has already taken shape.

Chapter 9

The Perfect Public Service Provider

Road to Perfection

The fifth stage of Lean is about aiming for perfection, where "perfection" might be defined as the state in which the organization finds itself after all deadly waste has been eliminated. Nobody makes any errors anymore, there are no more waits, documents are no longer shifted around, and monitoring is no longer necessary. Everything is of value in the eyes of the client.

The perfect Lean government has achieved the following: all individuals and other visitors enjoy the highest quality and security of life, delivered just-in-time and at the lowest cost, within the statutory parameters.

It should be clear to all that the perfect organization is an ideal that cannot realistically be achieved, so why do we continue to aim for perfection? In the case of for-profit organizations, it is to stay ahead of the competition. Their competitors are continually improving, and when they themselves stop evolving and improving, their competitors are sure to gain the edge. In the public sector, there's no such thing as competition, and, for a number of reasons, this is a missed opportunity.

There are several reasons why public organizations should nevertheless continue to improve and aim for perfection. An important reason to improve continually and strive for perfection in everything we do is the social responsibility to handle tax funds responsibly and not bother the public with unnecessary red tape.

It is also important to not lose sight of the political reality. Every two, four, or eight years, every democratic nation elects new public officials at all levels of government. This leads to a change in strategy and policy, followed by changes in legislation and the need to restructure processes. However, a specific incident also may prompt a legislator to change a Lean process and demand more stringent monitoring. A third reason is inherent to the organization—it is, simply put, fun to keep improving. It allows employees to grow in their roles and learn to use their talents as effectively as possible.

Lean and the Opportunities It Provides

Government organizations that work on the basis of the Lean principles can achieve excellent results, such as:

- Reducing lead time for welfare applications from six weeks to six days.
- Reducing lead time for disability welfare from four weeks to one day.
- Eliminating overprocessing by having a kaizen team integrate nine overlapping analog and digital filing systems of the Ministry of Justice into two electronic files.
- Reducing processing time for applications for facilities (for people with a disability) from 13 weeks to four days.
- Reducing the process of obtaining a parking permit from six weeks to one day; air-quality permits from 60 days to six days.
- Reducing the process of sending a confirmation of receipt from two weeks to the same day.
- Reducing the waiting lists in child and adolescent care facilities by 70%.
- Processing grant applications with 50% less processing time for civil servants.
- A city's annual budget report was brought back to half its size.
- The lead time for landfill permits was reduced from six months to one month.
- Facilities based on Lean processes, such as the express counter, were successfully introduced.
- The administrative burden for the public in the processing of tax exemption applications was reduced from eight hours to none.

The impact of these results directly benefits the public (in terms of reduced waiting times and administrative costs/burden) and the government organization itself (in terms of reduced processing times and a lower error rate).

Cases of Process Improvement

Solutions can sometimes be so simple that people wonder why they didn't think of them before. Below, we outline several cases that reflect the processes that must be completed to achieve perfection.

Invoice Processing

A water board orders equipment and services from third parties, and these companies then send invoices to the water board in hopes that they will be paid as soon as possible. In the old situation, the water board was not so prompt with its payments, the average terms of payment being 32 days. The water board received demands for payment for approximately 16% of all invoices, which involved additional work for the suppliers and the water board. The management board then decided to assign a kaizen team to analyze and improve the invoice payment process.

In addition to a large number of minor wastes and unnecessary steps, two main reasons for the long lead-time stood out:

1. The water board works on the basis of budget holders—i.e., heads of departments who monitor the budget. When their employees place orders, the invoice ends up on their desks to be initialed, having been forwarded by the invoice processing department. The bulk (more than 60%) of the total lead time of the invoice processing process is accounted for by these budget holders. The budget holder checks that the invoice is accurate and covered by the budget, while, in fact, the item ordered is already in use or has already served its use. The budget holder basically has no other choice than to sign the invoice, even if this means that his budget will be exceeded.

2. Suppliers that serve multiple departments of the water board send summary invoices that are subsequently sent to all the budget holders whose orders are listed on the invoice. The average waiting time per budget holder was ten days. If five different budget holders must sign the invoice, this equates to 50 days of lead time. While this was disadvantageous to many suppliers, it was the local florist that was most affected. His summary invoices needed to be signed by several budget holders, when, in fact, these invoices never exceeded $400.

The kaizen team managed to reduce average lead time from 32 days to 4.5 days (which equates to 85%). The change that saved the organization the most time was that the budget holders are no longer presented with invoices, but only see the actual orders (once they exceed a certain amount). The option of blocking orders allows them to monitor their budget and take action in time, whereas, with a system of invoices, it is already too late by the time they receive the invoice. Just removing the budget holders from the process alone has reduced lead time for processing invoices by more than 50%. With invoices, it is only necessary to verify that the service has been delivered and that the calculation is correct, a task that can easily be performed by administrative staff in the finance department.

A Municipality and Its Annual Budget

Government organizations dutifully set their budgets each year, a process that annually requires thousands of hours of work at every level of the organization. The final result is a large stack of paper full of reports outlining goals and a mishmash of indicators, key objectives, measures, targets, and goals. In a city with a population of 100,000, the total budget was 400 pages, which equated to four pages for every ten civil servants.

The budget included the following:

- 61 strategic objectives
- 160 subobjectives
- 309 indicators

Everything was measured; it was enough to make your head spin. The funny thing is that, although the budget for the coming year is almost 80% identical to that for last year, the municipal workers recalculated everything and added explanatory notes for all figures. The councillors, for whom the budget is ultimately intended, feel the thick stack of paper is difficult to read, and they find it hard to identify its main outlines. How can you manage a city that has as many as 61 strategic objectives? The members certainly felt this number could be reduced.

Next, a kaizen team analyzed the process and transformed the annual budget into a Lean product that was reduced by more than 50%. The number of measuring points and targets was reduced dramatically to the great satisfaction of the council members.

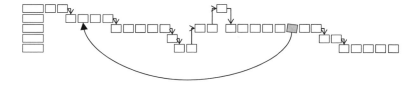

Figure 9.1 The decision is moved to the front of the process.

Welfare Applications

People might turn to the social services in a Dutch town to apply for welfare benefits to cover basic expenses, a facility that is provided only to those with no resources of their own. People who may have saved up money or own a boat or other luxury goods may complete this same process, but their applications are sure to be rejected. The relationship between employees in the social services and the members of the public applying for welfare is essentially a partnership: A person receives funds to cover his or her basic needs, on condition that he or she actively looks for a job. In this particular city, the person is required to start job application training the very next day, as well as having to take a series of competency tests and writing application letters.

A kaizen team was assigned to simplify the process of applying for welfare up to and including actual payment. This translates to less work for employees, less paperwork for the beneficiaries, and very short lead times. The team was extremely successful in its efforts. Administrative burden for the public was reduced to a minimum, as it later became evident that the city already had the majority of relevant data in its possession, either in its own systems or those of other services.

One of the team's remarkable findings was that 22% of applications were rejected. These rejections occurred in the latter stages of the process, toward the end. The team found that it is almost as costly to reject an applicant as it is to approve them, which led them to introduce a system where people were asked to answer a series of "knock-out questions" as soon as they appeared at the counter. The majority of the 22% were told during this preliminary screening process that they would not be eligible for welfare. This meant that it was no longer necessary to complete the rest of the process, reducing the processing time of rejected applications by 87% (Figure 9.1).

Lean and Politicians

Sometimes politicians are leading the improvement of government services. Mayors, councilmen, or high government officials who really believe in the power of Lean are a strong source of support for realizing a breakthrough in the quality of service. An almost ideal situation.

In those cases that politicians are not too interested in, it's the task of management to keep them informed and connected. Citizens will sooner or later become aware of some drastic improvements in service quality. Politicians will hear the positive remarks from the people. To avoid unnecessary suspicion, it is recommended that politicians be informed about planned improvements (or in some cases ask for approval or at least backup support). This is particularly true because along with all the positive effects, there may occur some troublesome incidents. It is important to be aware how politicians think. Their route for problem definition and coming to conclusions differs from civil servants. Both routes for analysis are based on evidence, but the evidence is different.

An example: A group of civil servants comes to a conclusion that in a certain process, a time-consuming check is redundant. The proof is that on average there is only one irregularity a year, and without serious side effects. The group decides, together with the department manager, to eliminate the check from the process. A year later, the group evaluates the impact and decides to continue the practice. One day an angry councilman calls the manager. He has heard that someone in the community is violating a regulation without action from the city. The manager claims that figures for the last year show that irregularities occur just once a year without serious ramifications, evidence based on measured facts. The councilman has his own evidence—what will happen when other councilmen hear about this? In addition, the councilman asks, do you know from whom I heard this? The councilman based his argument on the party's concern, its interests and the councilman's, rendering the measured facts meaningless (see Figure 9.2).

To avoid setbacks like this, inform politicians early and ask them for their support. Be aware of the difference between the political and official reality of analyzing problems and finding solutions.

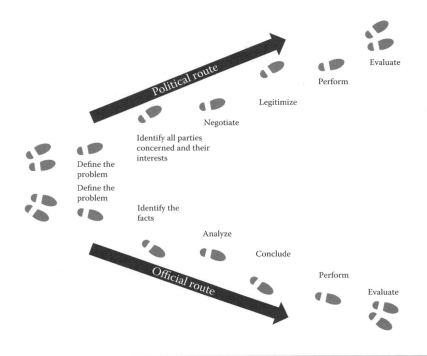

Figure 9.2   The difference between the problem-solving route of politicians and civil servants.

Chapter 10

The Process-Oriented Organization

Reorganization and Lean

Shared service centers, intermunicipal cooperation, mergers, and other forms of partnership involving government organizations remain popular. Ultimately, the majority of these initiatives are established because of the perceived efficiency benefits they provide. During the definition and design stages of these projects, a select group of people focuses extensively on the new organizational structure and the related issues, such as strategic objectives, core values, organizational tools, training, job descriptions, and resolving any policy disagreements. There is often not enough focus on processes and the way in which these processes run in the new organization, or it's simply a case of too little, too late. Oftentimes, processes are designed and imposed by a staff service, or an external party, such as a consultancy firm, whereby the large consultancy firms show a taste for information and communication technology (ICT).

Once the organization is ready to go live, everything may *seem* in place (on the face of it), but, in fact, all sorts of problems in the primary processes are likely to emerge, which were identified as mere details during the previous stages (that is, if they were identified at all) and not discussed any further. There are initial problems related to the organization's effectiveness: the basis of the service processes is not quite in place yet, the new building (if there is one) is not organized efficiently, or the old structure has not yet been changed. Errors that were common in the old organization are replicated in the new organization, which will inevitably have an impact on future processes. There are many issues to be resolved during this initial phase, yet, for some of these problems, it's too late because the building's layout can no longer be changed and the software has already been purchased. The staff is not involved in the organizational design (or became involved too late), and the predictable result is a lack of internal support, anger, frustration, and resistance.

As they get closer to the point where the partnership becomes a reality, the employees become increasingly nervous and ask questions about things that the project group regards as mere details, such as: What place will the process have in the new organization? What will my own place be? What systems will be required?

The project group has not focused enough on the details of the processes, whereas these details, which were not identified and implemented during the design phase (by the future users), result in a large number of "solvable problems" during the bumpy start-up period. However, what is even more serious is that the needs of the public were neglected. The focus was on the organization's own effectiveness, which has caused frustration among both the public and the administrators (Figure 10.1).

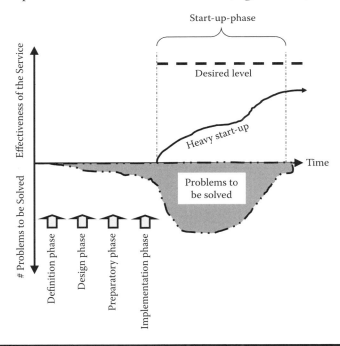

Figure 10.1 Start-up from a traditional reorganization.

This is a missed opportunity, as reorganization through these types of partnerships provides an excellent opportunity to improve organizational effectiveness. For example, when municipalities decide to collaborate, it's a good occasion to remove waste from the processes. Teams composed of employees of the organizations to be merged are assigned to integrate the two versions of the process into a single Lean process, incorporating the best features of both processes. This approach ensures ownership among the participants. They get to know each other while discussing each other's work and try to reach agreement on the new procedures. Additionally, this is also an effective way for the managers to get to know their team better.

Task-Oriented Versus Process-Oriented

Let's say a family of four went out for lunch together. The mother and the oldest son, Mike, both want to order pancakes, while the father and the youngest son, Luke, feel like having soup and a gourmet sandwich. Shortly after they have ordered their food, Dad and Luke are served their soup and sandwich. While they initially wait for a while until the other two are served their food, they eventually decide to tuck in, not wanting to let their food get cold. It is only after Dad and Luke have finished their lunch that the extremely irritated Mom and sulky Mike are served their pancakes.

This restaurant is designed from the perspective of efficiency. The kitchen and the preparation methods are designed to use the chefs' time as efficiently as possible, as they are responsible for the core business and are the highest-paid employees in the restaurant. In the current situation, tasty foods are prepared at the lowest possible costs. We are dealing with a task-oriented restaurant, one designed to perform tasks as efficiently as possible. The only downside is that it often makes for unhappy customers.

The key, therefore, is to structure our organization as efficiently as possible, allowing us to use our time as effectively as possible at the lowest possible cost. This is the inward-looking, "introvert" approach where the focus is on the costs. With this type of approach, the first question to ask is: "Who are my customers and how can I serve them most effectively?" Customers at this restaurant not only expect a high-quality dining experience, they also expect their food to be served at the same time as that of their dining companions. The purpose is not just to eat a tasty meal, but for the entire party to eat at the same time. Based on this question, both processes (let's call them the "pancake process" and the "soup and sandwich" process) are designed as effectively as possible and to work in conjunction with each other. In this situation, effectiveness is determined on the basis of customer needs. The next step is to ensure that the organization becomes as efficient as possible, without undermining effectiveness. Once this process is completed, the layout of the restaurant can be determined. With the focus being on customer value, the restaurant may decide to radically change the layout of its kitchen.

Vertical Start-Up

The first step in a reorganization process is usually to sketch an outline of the organization. Based on this framework, a job structure is then created, along with organizational tools and a blueprint of the future office. It is only after this procedure is completed that the processes are established. By that time, there is little scope left to design effective processes, as the design specifications mentioned above are cast in stone. The organization is designed on a task-oriented basis, with the objective being efficiency.

However, a process-oriented approach is more suited to a reorganization process where the focus is on creating value for the public. The first step in a process-oriented organizational approach is to identify the various processes and determine who the stakeholders are (i.e., citizen roles) and how value can be created as effectively as possible. The processes are designed to approach this level of effectiveness as closely as possible (Table 10.1). Based on the carefully outlined processes, it will then be possible to make an assessment of how the building should be designed and laid out. Instead of a project group or architect, the employees themselves prepare a solid proposal to determine who will be located where in the new building. Finally, this information can be used to create an "organizational rake" and to identify the duties, responsibilities, and authorities associated with specific positions. Then again, this no longer may even be necessary. The ideal situation (i.e., the vertical start-up) will be within closer reach now than would have been the case if a traditional approach had been used.

This ensures a sound basis (through the series of processes) as well as establishing a certain degree of ownership for the new procedures (Figure 10.2). This may help lower resistance to the reorganization process significantly, which is essential, as structural changes are challenging enough as it is.

Table 10.1   The Traditional and the Lean Sequence for Reorganizations

The Traditional Sequence	*The Process Oriented Approach*
• Make up a strategy for the organization	• Make up a strategy for the organization
• Design the outlines of the organization (i.e., the division into departments, defining who will be whose boss and the relocation of every individual in teams)	• Design or redesign the processes in a Lean way, linked with the strategy
	And, as a result:
• Give all departments and teams a location in the building	• Design the outlines of the organization
• Write down all job descriptions	• Organize the building for the designed processes in a logic way
And finally	• And, in the end:
• Design the processes	• Write down all job descriptions, if still necessary

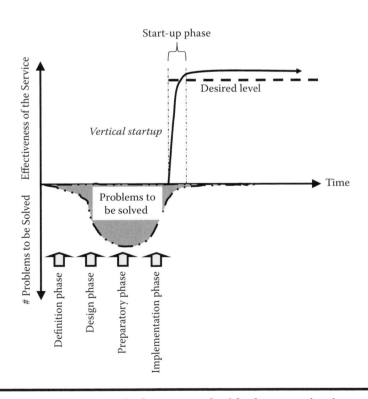

Figure 10.2   Vertical start-up; the ideal reorganization.

Case of the Social Services Department in the Town of Oldambt

There should be a solid foundation.

The practical case (see sections "Practice" in Chapter 7) is drawn from an intermunicipal social services department for Oldambt, a region in north-eastern Netherlands. The department's objective is to encourage unemployed residents of the Oldambt region to obtain gainful employment or become involved in the community in some other way. In the past, the apparent objective was to ensure that people received welfare benefits. While the number of welfare recipients in the Netherlands had steadily declined since 2000, the social services department in Oldambt actually saw an increase in the number of applications. Despite the high unemployment rate in the region, there continued to be job openings. In other words, it was essential for the department to switch to an alternative, more effective approach.

Who Ordered More Change?

With so many changes implemented within a short period of time, the department's staff was tired of having to adapt to these changes, and they were liable to resist yet another top-down plan for change. This prompted director Dick Vollbehr to decide on an alternative approach:

> *My employees are more likely to respond positively to a change process if they have some say in the new approach and, therefore, in the organization's structure. That means it is not only important to listen to what they have to say, but they should also be given the opportunity to design and implement the process themselves, based on the parameters specified.*

The consultants in the department spend a great deal of time organizing the welfare benefits, and the objective is to make the processes as smart as possible, ensuring that lead time for the applications will be significantly reduced and that the welfare officer will need to spend substantially less time on applications (i.e., reducing action time). As a result, there will be more time available to get clients back to work.

First, we need a solid foundation, which will allow us to focus on our job of getting customers back to work. At a later stage, we can then determine the most appropriate organizational structure.

Creating a Solid Foundation through Kaizen Teams

Several kaizen teams were established, comprising welfare officers, employees in the administrative section of the department, and staff members, who were assigned to improve the current processes. They were authorized to independently design a new process and make the necessary improvements. The teams were supervised by Dick Vollbehr the sponsor, who, along with his management team, created the assignments for the teams.

We drafted a project letter for each kaizen team containing the terms of reference and a quantifiable objective. These objectives involved dramatically reducing process lead times and ensuring that welfare officers would spend less time doing administrative work. The department's ultimate objective was to reduce both lead times and action times, ensuring better services for the customers. These objectives of the kaizen teams support the higher objective of getting more people back to work. By designing and implementing smarter processes, we gained time that we intended to use to help people find jobs.

Design and Action

Shortly after joining the social services department, I had an organizational structure in mind that I felt would be most effective. If I had decided to implement that right then and there, I would probably have encountered resistance. By assigning the teams to start out by optimizing the processes and then deciding on an appropriate organizational structure, we were able to achieve our goals as a department. Instead of resisting the project, my employees were actually very positive about it, and the teams even presented a proposal to improve the building's layout. We then implemented all the necessary changes. On the day the new processes were scheduled to be implemented, the walls were covered with large sheets of paper detailing the new process descriptions. We hardly experienced any problems at all.

Action Time Reduced by 50%

Once the kaizen teams' proposals have been implemented, the results in some cases even exceed the targets set out in the project letters. The time that officials still spend on processing welfare applications has been reduced by half, and lead time for basic welfare applications by 60%, well below the national average. Applications for certain types of disability welfare are processed within a single day, compared to the original lead time of seven working days. Waste, such as the large number of handovers and wait times and the double checks, have been removed from the processes, making them substantially more efficient.

Dick Vollbehr remarked:

> *What may be the most important improvement of all is that the time spent by officers on processing welfare applications has been reduced to a minimum. This will create a lot of additional time to help people find jobs. The amount of customer interaction has increased, and the fact that the employees designed and implemented the new processes themselves ensures maximum ownership. My entire team has been positive about the new processes, the method used to create them, and how they work in practice. Standardization of the processes allows us to focus more on reintegration.*

Fundamentals

A skeptic might say:

> *This sounds a little too good to be true. It's always a bit of a gamble allowing your employees this kind of freedom and responsibility. There are plenty of government organizations where people are simply marking time, happy with the way things are, and wary of change on account of previous, unsuccessful change processes. You can't just wave a magic wand and fix things. So, the output of your working groups won't be impressive, you'll find yourself entangled in a web of endless, pointless discussions, and there will be a lot of whining about more money and FTEs, and so on and so forth. Sometimes, all you can do is place the rat in the wheel and let it run.*

Whether or not employees can handle responsibility depends on the scope they are given. There is a limit to the mandate given to the kaizen teams allowed to design the new processes; clearly formulated project letters describe the parameters within which they must maneuver, in the form of a list of preconditions. New processes that don't meet these requirements are not implemented. Preconditions are set before the team begins its project rather than after they have completed it.

If a manager believes that the employees are just marking time, content with the status quo, he will find plenty of examples supporting his belief. Alternatively, he might wonder what gave rise to this situation in the first place, and whether he wants this to continue by letting people perform their established routines. If he continues placing rats in wheels, he'll find out he was right all along: "They're not doing what I want them to do; what a terrible attitude. We're dealing with a real cultural problem here."

Can you truly say that an organization is healthy when people don't really like working there and all they are ever allowed to do is what their boss tells them?

Chapter 11

Lean and Cost Savings

Benefit from Time Gained

How do you put the time you save through kaizen events to good use? The time saved only really works to your advantage if you have more time available for value creation, giving you the opportunity to perform valuable work for which there was previously no time. While the number of employees remains the same (as should the costs), time that was previously used to maintain the waste in a process is now used for valuable activities, which means you get more value for the same investment (i.e., in terms of time and money). However, if you do not end up creating more value, but do manage to eliminate waste and eventually win more time, how can you benefit from this to the fullest? The time you gain also could mean you require fewer staff and can create the same value while requiring less time and money; in other words, a leaner government.

We need to face the reality that all government agencies are compelled to cut costs from time to time, and there is often pressure to provide more services at a lower cost. The general consensus is that there are too many government workers, and in times of crisis when the corporate sector is hurting (such as in 2009), people will inevitably call for the government to cut costs. The federal government will then usually order lower-level governments to curb their spending, specifying a target amount with which governments must comply.

It's a shame that there are so few administrators and management boards in the government sector who regard it as their social duty to help create a leaner government. The reasons for cutting costs are usually considerably more mundane, specifically:

- A cost-savings target with which the government is required to comply, imposed by a higher level of government (e.g., the federal government as the main source of funding).
- Deficits created as a result of lower revenues or financial setbacks.

Cost-savings initiatives based on the reasons above are often not sustainable and focus only on short-term successes. During flush times, the organization will start growing again; however, the advantage for an organization of downsizing on its own initiative is that it will be able to do so at its own pace and according to its own plan.

The Government Unable to Cut Costs

As soon as there is a requirement to cut costs, many government organizations establish working groups ("downsize teams") composed of decision makers and controllers whose task is to assess opportunities for cost savings. In addition to generating more income by raising taxes, the group makes a list of all potential cost-saving opportunities and calculates the estimated savings. These are complex discussions because, during times of crisis revenues from building levies and the like are reduced, while corporate profits are down as well. It is very hard to make an estimate of these losses, and then there's the question of how the public will respond.

Parkinson's Law

Some believe that governments are actually *incapable* of cutting costs. The British economist Cyril Parkinson, for example, who investigated government organizations, published his findings (which he referred to as "laws") in slim, pseudoscientific volumes containing hilarious anecdotes about the government's inability to save costs. "*Work expands so as to fill the time available for its completion*" is the opening sentence of his book *Parkinson's Law* (Buccaneer Books, 1958). The economist "discovered" this law while analyzing procedures at the British Ministry of the Colonies, establishing that the number of government workers employed at the ministry had been steadily increasing over the years. What was remarkable, however, was that this had nothing to do with the size of the colonies; in fact, as the British Empire crumbled after World War II, the number of government workers at the Ministry of the Colonies actually continued to increase. This led Parkinson to conclude that the size of an administrative organization depends on the scope of the work performed by that organization. He found that the type of work someone performed effectively did not matter, as they simply continued performing their work based on the time available.

The enduring popularity of *Parkinson's Law* can be credited to the fact that people sense that it's the truth, as we have all witnessed practical examples that demonstrate just what he was trying to prove.

Parkinson noticed the phenomenon, looked for facts that would support his observation, and then promptly declared it a law. Still, a law only qualifies as such if there are no facts to the contrary. This is not the case, as some government organizations have indeed been reduced in size over the years. A case in point is Denmark, where government reform resulted in a dramatic reduction in the number of municipalities, and county boundaries were redrawn, after which there were only five regions remaining.

What makes it so hard in the public sector to use the time gained through such processes? The answer is that there are forces that attempt to prevent real cost savings on personnel; people will always try to protect their own position, security, and status. Not every manager will allow substantial downsizing in his department as a result of smarter, more efficient processes. The size of the team under the manager's supervision gives him status, and, in addition, the size of his department provides him with the reassurance that his position is secure. In fact, it is very possible that despite the Lean processes implemented by a department, which save considerable time, no new value-creating activities are performed, and staff in the department works exactly the same number of hours as they did before the improvements were implemented. This manager and his department bear out Parkinson's law: "*Work expands so as to fill the time available for its completion.*" This type of behavior is particularly prevalent in large government organizations where there is a sharp division of duties, departments feel little affiliation with the organization as a whole, and employees are particularly unaware of their social responsibility.

Frugality Is Punished

Another force is the lack of necessity to improve processes and perform more services at a lower cost. This is often related to the fact that the requirement to improve is imposed by the federal government, which tells the lower-level governments how much they are to save. Government organizations that experience this pressure do not feel they own this process and try to shirk their responsibility or resist in other ways—for example, by presenting data on the improvements they supposedly implemented, when, in fact, there is no sign of any improvement at all.

On the contrary, the higher-level government that forces lower-level governments to cut cost when times are lean, actually *rewards* them for spending the entire budget during times of prosperity. In many countries, organizations that demonstrate that they can provide the same services for less are often "punished" by the government through budget cuts. If an organization does not use up its budget in time, it receives less funding the following year. The perverse result is that, when good times are about to come to an end and the budgets haven't been used up, governments will come up with ways to spend the money before the end of the year.

A third alternative to cut costs is through a reduction in force (RIF). Staff is laid off without any measures being taken to reduce waste or save time on processes. This temporary reduction in force will be more than compensated for in the future. The result is a discrepancy in the workforce that would look like a saw tooth if it were represented in a diagram (i.e., a low in the workforce is followed by a peak, which is always slightly higher than the previous peak). This has caused the number of employees to increase over the years. You might make an analogy with overweight people who have undergone liposuction. The fact that their fat was removed doesn't necessarily mean that they have changed their eating patterns.

Cost-Saving Strategies

When it comes to cutting costs, government organizations have a number of options. There is a group of cost-cutting measures of which the public will feel the impact virtually right away, and a group of which the impact will not be as immediate.

Less for Less

In this alternative, certain public facilities will be cancelled. The reasoning behind this decision is somewhat crude: "Our town currently has three sports centers. How much will we save if we close one of them?" In reality, it remains to be seen whether this will save the municipality any money at all in the short term because it is hard to fire the people who manage the centers (they will continue to receive pay), and the maintenance of the sports center will continue to require funding until a new buyer comes along. Also, it is important not to underestimate the impact of a vacant building on the neighborhood where the sports center is located.

Another example is reducing the amount of funding paid to individuals by reducing grants and benefits, while a third example is to cut back on expenses related to the management and maintenance of public space— e.g., by cutting the grass or cleaning the streets less frequently.

These are all examples of cutbacks which the public will see or be impacted by immediately or in the longer term, and ultimately this means that less value will be created for the public and their tax money.

The Same for Less

Another option is to eliminate jobs without undermining the volume and quality of the services; that is to say, performing the same work with fewer people and for less money. A less radical version of this is a hiring freeze, and as a result of regular staff turnover this will eventually reduce the number of employees. A more drastic alternative is to lay off 10 to 20% of the staff, based on the assumption that the remaining employees will be able to take on the workload of their redundant coworkers. Managers who follow this approach use the inverse of Parkinson's law: *There is always something to be gained by winning back the time allotted for a specific task.* In addition to the demoralizing effect this approach has on the organization, there are also a number of side effects.

These effects are based on the assumption that government workers spend a significant part of the day doing nothing and the time that a group of government workers is idle can be filled with the duties of another government worker, who then will have nothing to do at all. This latter employee, therefore, can be dismissed. Beside the fact that it's not always easy to lay off government workers, the assumption is not always accurate either, as many government workers, in fact, are busy all the time. This means that, if the workforce is reduced, the quality of the services will most likely suffer, and people will notice that lead times have increased.

More for Less

Like their counterparts in the corporate sector, government workers are simultaneously busy creating value and maintaining waste. Although the same service—or even an improved version—can be provided with fewer staff, the processes will first need to be rid of waste. As we have seen in the previous chapters, kaizen teams can radically reduce action times in processes by using simple Lean tools and principles. If the action time has been reduced for a large number of processes, services can be provided with fewer staff, while the quality of the processes and services, in fact, has been enhanced (i.e., shorter lead times and greater accuracy). In other words, more for less.

Government organizations that are seeing their workforce shrink while at the same time creating more value have achieved this through the following success factors:

- As a manager or director, you should not wait for targets imposed by a higher-level government, but rather take a proactive approach. You should consider it your public duty to make the organization leaner; be sure you choose "more for less."
- Do not choose to eliminate a portion of the workforce all at once, but rather take a gradual approach. Improve the processes and gain time in the process; let people go gradually, over a longer period of time, by letting go of temporary workers and by allowing older employees to retire early.
- Outsource processes, including employees, to private-sector partners and establish a customer–supplier relationship with these partners.

In addition, national governments should consider how they might reward, rather than punish, lower governments that have not used up their budget. One option would be to allow them to invest the remaining funds in infrastructure, in supporting economically disadvantaged people, or in innovation. The basic requirement should always be that the public should not suffer from the impact of budgets remaining unspent.

Reduce, Then Improve?

Managers who were hired specifically to make a government organization leaner sometimes have doubts as to what approach they should use.

Ownership is a key aspect of the Lean principles, and, if you intend to downsize your organization, you will first need to win time by improving processes, after which the workforce then can be reduced. The manager in our example will need to consider very carefully how he intends to use the time he gained back. People at certain levels of the organization will not be willing to return the time they gained.

Another, tougher approach is to start out by eliminating jobs, after which you will be forced to make your processes smarter because the workload will have increased so much that every little bit of time you gain is welcome. The downside of this system is that it has a demoralizing effect on staff, who will be more inclined to call in sick. Naturally, the pressure described above also could be counterproductive. How would you even find the time to improve processes? Who would have time to participate in kaizen teams?

The Turkey

The key question is: How can you improve through Lean when the government is pressuring you to cut costs? While kaizen teams may be an excellent way to mobilize employees, it's not realistic to think that they will willingly cooperate in their own redundancy (Figure 11.1). It's akin to asking the turkey to help you set the Thanksgiving dinner menu. Top-down cutbacks cause people to resist or cower in a corner until it's safe to come out again. On the face of it, Lean and cost cuts do not seem like a successful union. Lean is designed to eliminate waste and maximize value, rather than to reduce costs.

Nevertheless, there are ways to use Lean for process improvement, even under these unfavorable conditions. There are government organizations

Figure 11.1

where the employees are committed to creating a lean organization, even though they know that it will lead to workforce reduction over time. The management can foster that commitment by explaining the downsizing process when they are first implementing the cutbacks—e.g., how many people will be affected and in what departments. If layoffs are announced unexpectedly and jobs will be eliminated within a short period of time, it's best not to make the connection with Lean. However, if people are let go over a longer period of time and some take early retirement, combined with a hiring freeze, the implementation of Lean need not necessarily meet with resistance; on the contrary, it may actually reduce the impact of the cutbacks on staff morale. Their reasoning is that if cutbacks are inevitable, they would actually like to have a say in it. In addition, it is important that the management does not let staff wait too long until the expected measures are implemented. You should start by identifying the processes that need to be improved and allow employees to play an active role in this process.

Select a group of employees who will form full-time kaizen teams based on voluntary registration. This group of kaizen leaders will receive training in Lean methods and in dealing with group-dynamic phenomena, such as resistance and a loss of self-esteem. Next, establish the kaizen teams that will be responsible for improving the processes, headed by trained kaizen leaders. Preferably, you should not put people on the kaizen team who are already expected to be laid off, as they will no longer have the courage or strength to contribute.

Time gained as a result of improved processes must immediately lead to a reduction in force. As a manager, you should provide absolute transparency by publishing regular reports on progress and results.

Chapter 12

Workplace Organization Based on the 5Ss

Search Time: 30 Seconds Maximum

Whenever improvements are made, the emphasis is usually on making processes more logical and eliminating waste. However, the physical work environment also has a major impact on the effectiveness of processes to the point where an unorganized, messy workplace can be a source of error, disturbances, and accidents. The reason is the presence of redundant materials, items that are not stored in a permanent place, and a lack of standard procedures. As a result, irregularities in the work process are not visible, or are only seen too late, or too much time is wasted looking for the right documents or files, or even something as simple as a stapler. Workspaces can be organized as garages or as supermarkets. Garages are enclosed areas where only the owner knows where anything is located (or at least he thinks he does), whereas supermarkets are accessible to all and are logically designed to ensure that customers can see where everything is located.

Behavioral change in organizations is difficult to accomplish and requires a lot of conversation and persuasive power. An easier way to change behavior is to adapt the environment, because people are affected by their work environment. For example, people behave differently in a doctor's waiting room than they do in an airport waiting lounge, just as they won't act the same in a high school locker room as they would in a hospital. In an area where cigarette butts, apple cores, and other junk are scattered across the floor,

Figure 12.1   A messy workplace

people are more likely to dispose of their trash as well. In other words, same people, different environment, different behavior. A messy and chaotic work environment incites a different type of behavior than a clean, well-organized office (Figure 12.1). The quality of the environment reveals something about the quality of the work and work processes. A well-organized workplace has a positive impact on the quality of the work; people make fewer errors and spend less time waiting and looking for lost items.

The following are characteristics of a well-organized workplace:

■ There is no clutter.
■ It is immaculately clean and neat.
■ The paperwork required is minimal and simple.
■ It never takes more than 30 seconds to find items or information.
■ It never takes more than 30 seconds to store away items or information.
■ There are clear standard procedures in place.
■ The workplace is so neatly organized that any irregularities are immediately noticeable.

The Practical Method

5S is an effective way to organize the workplace in such a way that it positively affects the mood of the users. Having its origins in Japan, 5S describes how to create a friendly, stimulating work environment in which irregularities are instantly visible. The 5S philosophy states that working in a chaotic environment leads to chaotic behavior, or, conversely, we can change our behavior for the better by changing our environment. 5S is divided into five phases, all of which start with an S:

1. Sort
2. Set in order
3. Shine
4. Standardize
5. Sustain

The purpose of 5S is to create the **perfect workspace**, one where:

■ No accidents ever happen; a safe workplace where you never slip or trip.
■ No one is ever sick because they work in such a pleasant, safe, and secure environment.
■ No errors are made because people are well trained and procedures are solid and standardized.
■ There is no waste; processes run waste-free and have short lead times.

An explanation follows.

First S: Sort

Distinguish between documents, office materials, etc., that are necessary and those that are redundant. All materials and documents should be critically assessed: do you need them or can they be thrown out? Discard what is unnecessary or auction it off to your colleagues. Stick a red tag (Figure 12.2) on any items that are attached to the floor or wall, so that everyone will know that it's redundant.

Don't hesitate to overhaul everything; you should not only remove redundant items from the cabinets, but actually empty the entire cabinet and review every single item in it. Do we need this? If not, throw it in the trash, and, when in doubt, do the same. At the end of this exercise, your cabinet may have less than half the contents it did before, but since even half-full cabinets will be filled to the brim again in just several months, it's recommended that you dramatically reduce the amount of cabinet space

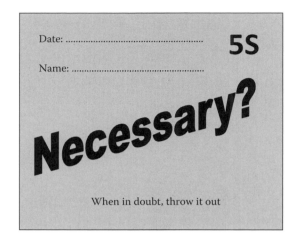

Figure 12.2

because the less storage space you have, the less you will be likely to hoard things.

Any items lying around of which it is unclear whether they are needed in that particular space must be relegated to the "auction space." At the end of phase 1, the group assesses any items in this area for usefulness, after which it's either throw them out for good or find a permanent place to store them (Figure 12.3).

Figure 12.3

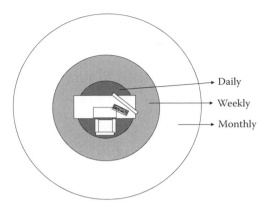

Figure 12.4   5S radius: Everything gets a proper place depending on the frequency of use.

Second S: Set in Order

Any items that survived phase 1 are assessed to see how often they are used. The higher the frequency of use of items and documents, the more the workplace will resemble the stable, visualized workspace. Items used on a daily basis are stored close to the workstation, items that are used weekly a little farther away, and items that you require only once a month or so are stored in a central location in the department.

Along with your coworkers, set the 5S radius used to determine the correlation between the frequency of use and the distance to the workstation (Figure 12.4). More than half of all documents produced are stored in more than one location, and sometimes the documents are stored only a couple of feet away from each other. It is worth considering storing these documents in one central location.

Likewise, it is important to organize all items visually in such a way that all users can see them at a glance and take out and put back what is necessary. Examples of visualization of permanent locations include shadow boards, lines and squares on the floor, and tags on cabinet shelves.

A list is maintained to record which items are necessary and which aren't, including who will ensure that the item will be given a permanent location in the near future.

Third S: Shine (Cleaning = Inspection)

Cleaning and tidying are important in ensuring that the workplace looks good, such as, when clients visit. A clean work environment will inspire users to keep it clean. In the spirit of the 5Ss, an added benefit of cleaning and tidying is that all kinds of irregularities are identified during this exercise. Many bikers, for example, prefer to clean their own motorcycle, as that allows them to discover any possible tears, oil leaks, and the like. In that sense, cleaning is a form of inspection. Furthermore, it was recently demonstrated that there is a direct correlation between a clean work environment and absenteeism, particularly in office environments. That doesn't mean that office workers will need to vacuum their own offices from now on, but regularly cleaning cabinets, desks, and the floor can help identify irregularities, such as forgotten action points or documents that haven't been properly filed away.

Fourth S: Standardize

The purpose of the fourth and fifth Ss is to keep up the first three Ss and maintain control of the process by doing everything according to fixed procedures. Standardization is seriously underestimated; it is generally associated with instructions and procedures, as though that's any guarantee that people will actually start working according to these instructions. As a general rule, the more work instructions there are, the smaller the chance that they will actually be followed and the more challenging it is to keep everything up to date. There are far more effective forms of standardization, such as visual control tools that actually control behavior. If you park your car at the grocery store, you also are not given any operating instructions, but instead your behavior is directed by your environment (e.g., through demarcations on the floor, signs, etc.) For more information on this subject, see Chapter 8, Standardization and Compliance. Standardization is something you do for your coworkers rather than for yourself. They must also be able to find anything within 30 seconds.

An example of a standard is a series of steps that are performed to grant permits or handle complaints. Alternatively, standards can be created to purchase and store office materials and equipment—e.g., minimum and maximum stock levels. To achieve even the slightest efficiency benefit, people often stock up on items for several years. However, not only must all these items be stored, they may actually become unusable because of a changed logo, etc.

Fifth S: Sustain

Everyone demonstrably complies with the standard until there is a better alternative. Maintaining these standards is a matter of discipline, and the likelihood that the new, organized work environment will be maintained successfully depends on the ease with which the employees can keep it up. If complex standards have been created to keep the workspace organized and facilitate processes, people will soon look for easy alternatives that may be less effective or even unsafe, but somehow easier to implement. The level of workplace organization can be measured by conducting audits (see Appendix E) in the actual workspace.

Although there are certainly opportunities for improvement in the office, you might ask yourself how useful it is to start 5S before the processes have been analyzed and improved. The answer to that question depends on the physical work environment: is it messy, is there a lot of clutter, is it chaotic? If this is the case, and the teams improve the processes without properly analyzing the workplace, there is a significant chance that the result of the improvement will be lost over time. In that case, the basic conditions are not in order, resulting in new waste despite people's best efforts. In other words, documents will get lost in the mess and people will undoubtedly make errors. The celebrated Italian educator Maria Montessori said that a messy desk is a messy head, or, to translate it to Lean terms, if the environment is messy or even chaotic, the processes are likely to be the same.

The perfect workplace becomes a reality, as 5S ensures that:

- All items and tools in the office have a permanent, logical place, ensuring that search times are reduced.
- Once the workspace is in order, any defects and irregularities can be identified and eliminated much sooner, thereby preventing waste.
- The workspace has been standardized and visualized such that the behavior of all individuals involved (both members of the public and employees) is positively affected.
- The employees are mobilized to start implementing improvements.
- 5S is a practical method that leads to visible results and incites people to continue the improvement process well beyond the initial exercise.

Preparation for 5S

Office workers tend to organize their workstation as they see fit, and there's usually no particular plan behind it. As a result, two employees that perform the same work may have organized their individual workstations very differently. An office worker's desk is in a "gray area" between organizational

Figure 12.5

property and private property, as illustrated by the family pictures and decorations that people use to personalize their workstations. The closer you get to the employee's chair, the more personal their environment gets. This may lead to problems, because the key question we ask in 5S is: *Is it necessary or redundant?*

During the "clean-out," the entire office is overhauled—all cabinets, drawers and other storage areas are opened and emptied, and the contents are reviewed. There are some items that employees consider personal, such as one particular drawer of a desk or their own cabinet, and they might get quite upset if others go through these items and conclude that many of them are redundant. As the supervisor of a clean-out, it is a good thing to encourage people to take action, but you need to make sure not to go too far. For each step you take and for each component of 5S, you should ask yourself if this will help you reduce waste. It's not about cleaning for the sake of cleaning, but rather about increasing organizational effectiveness. The 5S supervisor asks the questions and makes suggestions, but ultimately it's the employee who makes the decisions (Figure 12.5).

5S Is a Team Endeavor

It is generally better to start 5S in the office by organizing and visualizing *shared* workspaces, such as desks used by more than one person, and shared cabinets and areas, such as the copy room, the filing room, and the digital workstation. Assigning a permanent, visualized place to someone's personal stapler, when the user never really has to look for it, will only lead to unnecessary resistance. 5S is a team endeavor, but, unlike with kaizen teams, participation is not voluntary. When someone absolutely does not want to be part of a kaizen team, it's best that they not be admitted as a member. The implementation of 5S, by contrast, affects the entire department, which means that everyone gets involved, including the managers—in fact, *especially* the managers, as they have to lead by example in organizing the workspace. There are always people who regard the exercise as silly and pointless. More often than not, however, these are employees who are invested in keeping the work and work environment nontransparent, or those who are chaotic by nature. These people's workstations typically resemble their garage or attic at home. Experience has shown that employees in organizations feel differently about the usefulness of 5S. There are those who welcome the fact that the workplace is finally getting the attention it deserves; you should cherish these people and give them a key role in the project by, say, letting them participate in a 5S team, which are preparing and leading clean-outs. Then there is a large group of those who are still on the fence. They would like to believe that it's useful, but they need a little coaxing. These people participate in the exercise out of curiosity. If you do things right, they might even get excited, particularly when they see visible improvements.

Starting with 5S also means continuing with 5S; it basically never ends. It's a matter of continuing to aim for the perfect workplace, one without waste. However, it is often difficult to prevent people from slipping up. How do you ensure that 5S is more than just a fad, but something that will be embedded in the organization? While starting 5S initially costs a lot of energy, having to start the process all over again after initial failure costs twice as much energy because at that point employees have already experienced that maintenance can be tricky. The challenge now is to persuade them to start the process over again.

Starting 5S: The Clean-Out

Select the areas that are to be given the 5S treatment. A room should be selected based on some of the following criteria:

- The area is frequented by the public (e.g., municipal service desk, social services department, etc.).
- There is a proven need to organize the workplace (e.g., because there's too much clutter).
- The workplaces are shared by multiple employees.
- The majority of these employees are not happy with the current state of the workplace.
- There is a reasonable chance of a positive effect.

In order to maximize the result of a clean-out, the exercise must be carefully prepared. This helps prevent confusion among the employees involved in the clean-out and ensures that they will not need to look for detergents and the like. To sum it up:

- Make sure the department has a clear **purpose** for 5S. The head of the department is responsible for effectively translating the 5S goals of the management into goals for his/her department. These goals may either be related to the exercise itself or to the result. An example of a task related to the exercise might be drafting a minimum number of proposals for improvement (see Chapter 6, section "Everyday Lean" and Appendix D) that he/she would like to see, or the score achieved through the 5S audit (see Appendix E). Result targets are about reducing waste, reducing the lead time of administrative processes, and saving space. The goals may relate either to this year or next.
- The head of the department starts the clean-out with a brief introduction, in which he/she explains the importance of a well-organized and visualized workplace for the department and for each individual employee. The 5S team can help the head of the department to write his/her opening speech. It is essential that both the members of the 5S teams and the heads of the departments have completed 5S training, so that they know exactly what they're talking about.
- Send an invitation to all employees that clearly explains both 5S and the clean-out and that includes the day's program. If applicable, the invitation should state that everyone should show up in work clothes because they will be participating in a practical exercise.
- Divide the total work area into smaller sections, then divide all employees into groups of two to four across these sections. Make sure that people organize their own workplace rather than those of others. Although it may be fun to throw someone else's stuff away, this may lead to trouble

later on. Add people to the group who do not work in this part of the building on a daily basis, but who are still inconvenienced by the way the room is organized and the way the processes are currently operated. This can potentially lead to a fresh perspective on the situation.

■ Before every clean-out, a brief presentation is held explaining the exercise. Employees are curious to see how things will go during the day. Make sure to also inform people of what will happen after the clean-out is completed, but keep it short (30 minutes maximum), as employees expect this to be a practical day.

■ Ensure that everything is ready. For example:
  - Cleaning materials (e.g., brooms, buckets, detergents, sponges)
  - Enough trash cans (plus a shredder for documents containing sensitive information)
  - Red 5S tags (Figure 12.2)
  - "Auction lists" (Listing who gives what article a permanent visualized place)
  - Cameras
  - A tag printer to tag the cabinet shelves
  - Colored tape to temporarily section off parts of the area
  - Audits (Appendix E)

■ Draw up rules for the filing policy (how long should specific documents be saved, etc., how should they be submitted to the filing department, can they be sent electronically, etc.?).

■ Make it possible to convert print documents to electronic format by having them scanned and tagged on the spot.

■ Make sure that all waste is separated. Toners and ink, for example, produce chemical waste, but this also includes other high-risk waste, such as documents containing sensitive information.

■ Ensure that full paper containers are properly removed, as clean-outs tend to produce tons of paper waste.

■ Make clear in advance that the clean-out is first and foremost about implementing the first three Ss, in order to prevent someone not achieving anything all day except to go through three folders. Leave the folder level for later.

In order to make the team members aware of good workplace organization, it helps to help them experience the current condition of the workplace (Figure 12.6). This can be accomplished by instructing the groups to take photographs of chaotic situations in the workplace or of redundant items.

Figure 12.6   Before the clean-out

Figure 12.7   After the clean-out

A 5S audit list (see Appendix E) can be used to assess the workplace on a quantitative level. This ensures that it will remain possible to measure progress at a later stage of the 5S process.

Clean Desk and the Paperless Office

In the office world, 5S tends to be associated with *Clean Desk* Policy, a policy whereby, at the end of the workday, there may no longer be any paper on the desk, but everything must be stored in folders, cabinets, and drawers. Organizations that operate the Clean Desk Policy do so because there is a risk that documents containing sensitive information may end up in the wrong hands. In addition, it may be convenient for the cleaning service, as they will have more easy access to surfaces. Clean Desk has nothing to do with eliminating deadly losses in the workplace; you can also have a clean desk if, at the end of the day, you gather all the paper on your desk, stack it together, and dump it in a cabinet.

Organizations with a virtually *paperless office* can appear to be well organized at first glance. There are advantages to working in a paperless environment and performing all tasks electronically because, if the system is well organized, there will only be one version: the most current one. However, operating a paperless office can present problems. Right before a meeting everyone is usually gathered around the printer, as all participants in the meeting want to have a hard copy of the agenda. Therefore, paperless is not necessarily the perfect solution for the organized office workplace. Although it may be well organized physically, electronically it may be a different story altogether. Organizations that make the transition to an all-electronic, paperless environment and forget to organize this digital workplace according to the 5S principles end up creating a digital garage with a proliferation of electronic folders and files, the total mass of which may eventually exceed the terabyte barrier (10^{12} bytes).

A Practical Restart

In addition to being an effective method for workplace organization, 5S also is useful for shaking things up. Improving processes while the work environment remains chaotic may lead everyone to quickly revert to the old situation. This is why it may be sensible to spend several days organizing the workplace using the 5Ss. A major clean-out in which everyone participates may be the start of some significant improvements. Instead of going on corporate retreats and designing models, the process is about literally cleaning up the workplace. This makes 5S a valuable practical tool for leaders looking to launch a change program in their department or organization.

The Devil Is in the Detail

For an organization that has recently relocated, the start-up phase can be difficult and drawn out. This tough beginning is not always the result of organizational design errors. While there may be nothing wrong with the overall plan, it's the details where things tend to go awry. To name a few mundane examples: a lack of correct e-mail addresses or telephone connections, non-activated USB ports, confusion as to who is located where in the building, and who stores what information where. Although these may seem like mere details, they are likely to have repercussions and can have a crippling effect on the organization's effectiveness and efficiency. If the organization is relocating to another building, or within the same building, employees have some control over the layout and design of their new workplace. Based on the 5S principles, the building and the workplace can be laid out as conveniently as possible, preferably combined with a redesign of the work processes. This ensures a sense of ownership among the new users of the building, and they will be more likely to remember the details. The result is that the workplace is now designed for its employees to work as effectively as possible, keeping the number of deadly wastes to a minimum.

Digital 5S

Servers and hard disks represent electronic storage areas where anyone in an organization can virtually walk in and out and store a wide variety of data. These servers and hard disks contain both old and new files as well as identical documents in different locations. Users give these folders and documents names that make sense to them: their own name, their initials, a date (e.g., the date of the first draft), or a name of a case they are working on. This means that valuable time is lost in the organization due to people looking for information in vain. Employees are liable to make errors when they open the wrong file or an outdated file.

Try the following experiment. Get out a stopwatch and record the time it takes you to search for a particular document. Make sure you don't pick any files you organized yourself, as this is not likely to present any problems.

The digital workplace can be organized on the basis of the 5S principles as well. As part of the clean-out, employees check their personal hard drive (provided it is accessible) and the documents they use that are stored on public drives. Let a group of employees make a list beforehand of the rules for the structure of folder and document names. It is important to keep it short and simple and ensure that the subject can be identified at a glance. Create a filing policy stating which documents must be kept for what period of time. Be sure to include that there is no statutory or legal minimum storage period, and that, for example, documents that have not been used in the past two years are automatically deleted or stored in a separate zone. This "zone" might be a back-up disk that will be retained for several months.

The Digital 5 Ss:

The first S: **Sort**—You should distinguish between necessary and redundant files. Each employee goes through his or her files and determines what can be deleted and what is essential. Do not open and analyze every file, but work on the basis of a number of basic rules:

■ Use a software tool to analyze whether certain documents are stored in multiple places, then verify which one is correct and delete the other files.
■ Documents that have not been opened for more than a specific number of weeks/months can be deleted (unless otherwise provided by law).
■ Remove any software that is not used.

The second S: **Set in order**—Give each file a logical place in order to prevent that any time is wasted searching. Give folders a logical place.

■ Together with your team, determine what the folder structure (i.e., the "tree") will look like. Carefully consider this "order principle;" try to organize in a process-oriented way as much as possible to ensure that the logical process order is clear from the folder structure.
■ Ensure that frequently used folders and files are not buried somewhere deep inside the tree structure. Do not use too many layers.
■ Move files to the correct folder (i.e., one with a logical name). Make sure there are fewer than 10 to 15 files per folder, in order to facilitate the search process.
■ Use multiple types of icons (or colors) for folders to specify the type of file.

There is special software available for Document Management Systems (DMS) that registers documents using a logical, standardized name and some additional details, such as document type (e.g., policy document, report, photos, presentation, etc.) and status (e.g., "draft," "under review," or "final"). Documents can easily be found if they're tagged, and you can learn how to tag them effectively by first understanding how the search process works.

The perfect DMS no longer requires a tree structure, as it features a search screen (similar to Google™) that allows you to find anything, unless you haven't used a logical tag.

The third S: **Shine**—Cleaning can be a very physical process; clean your computer and keyboard and remove any food residues. Electronic cleaning is about assigning documents standardized names. During this exercise, employees may come across all kinds of documents that are still awaiting action. As before, it is important to remember here that *cleaning = inspection.*

- Determine the standard for document names prior to the exercise.
- Automate the cleaning process by ensuring that the archive manager periodically deletes specific folders after a certain date has been exceeded or moves them to a digital red-tag zone by pressing a button.

The fourth S: **Standardize**—Together with your team, create a method to make the digital workplace free of waste.

- Prepare a cleaning plan that specifies how frequently cleaning should take place.
- Develop a system where anyone can easily indicate that a file has an incorrect or illogical name.
- Train everyone in the use of these standards.

The fifth S: **Sustain**—Make sure that everyone sticks with the system.

- Audit the digital workplace.
- Use visual indicators to show the performance of 5S. This might be in the form of diagrams showing the total amount of mass taken up by all files, the number of files per person, the number of files with the same name, and a Pareto graph showing the age of the files.

Some organizations block access to personal hard drives (such as the C drive) and a number of shared drives in order to force all employees to use the general hard drive and the associated tree structure. Recall that storage of information is similar to a system of interconnected vessels. If the fluid is pressed down into one column and subsequently locked, the level of the other columns will increase, including that of unwanted "columns," such as paper files and even USB sticks or another general hard drive not intended for that purpose. Find ways to make the storage space user-friendly on the basis of a tree structure used by the employees themselves. The more attractive the required path is, the smaller the chance that employees will choose other storage options.

Practical Case: Tax Department of the Municipality of Dordrecht

The status of workstations in the department may be a reason to start a 5S process. Arri Hartog, the head of the tax department of the Dutch municipality of Dordrecht (population: 120,000) thought it was about time.

> *Before you start improving work processes, you need to make sure the workplace is in order. A messy environment has a significant impact on the quality of the work performed, which leads to deadly waste. Our employees felt that there was not enough cabinet space— folders were lying on top of cabinets or right behind them. People were stacking documents inside the cabinets, which sometimes made it hard to find them.*

One day the system was down for maintenance and it was the perfect opportunity for the clean-out (Figure 12.8 and Figure 12.9). The department was divided into sections, and the employees were divided into small teams across these sections. Obviously, managers participated in the clean-out as well.

Figure 12.8 Before the clean-out

Figure 12.9   After the clean-out

The exercise started with a brief explanation of the 5S principles, after which an overview was provided of the current situation through pictures and the 5S audit (Appendix E). The average audit score was around 40 points (the maximum score is 100). Hartog remarked:

> *A little hesitantly, we started out separating the first S (**Sort**) by carefully removing some items from the cabinets. But once someone in the team took the initiative and the managers showed the way as well, we soon got into it.*

All items were removed from the cabinets, and the team assessed whether they were really necessary in the workplace (Figure 12.10). Cabinets that were no longer useful were removed from the department, so as to prevent them from becoming full again just several months later. The more storage space there is available, the more likely people will be to hoard.

Sure, there are always people who feel a clean-out is a useless exercise, but you will find that those are inevitably the people who are happiest when their workplace looks like a garage. However, there are also employees who regard the clean-out as an opportunity to order their workspace and reorganize it in a logical way (Figure 12.11). The clean-out is a team endeavor, as 5S focuses on shared areas. Whether or not someone cleans out their private drawer is up to them.

Figure 12.10

Figure 12.11

Logical Organization

As the afternoon progressed, people were asked to consider the logic of the way the desks and cabinets were organized. Based on the outcome of the work processes, the department subsequently switched to a more logical system (Figure 12.12).

At the end of the workday, the teams presented the results of the clean-out to each other and explained how the level they had reached could be sustained (in accordance with the fifth S, **Sustain**).

Figure 12.12

Appendix A: Process Activity Sheet

Process Activity Sheet		*Process: Receipt for an Appeal*					
No.	*Activity*	*V/W*	*Action Time*	*Lead Time*	*WIP*	*Process Participants*	*Remarks*
1	Appeals through a letter					Financial organization	
2	Brings mail to the mail room	T	4			Mail room	
3	Sorts mail per department and puts it in a mailbag	T	10	0.25		Mail room	
4	Delivers the mailbag to secretary	T	25			Mail room	
5	Registers the appeal and postmarks with date	OK/O	2			Secretary Legal Dept.	
6	Puts the appeal in the mail tray of the assistant	T	5	0.1		Secretary Legal Dept.	
7	Empties his mail tray and brings mail to his desk	T/U	7		4	Legal assistant	Assistant is out of office 40% of time
8	Reads the appeal superficially and stores in mail tray on his desk	R/T/U	6	4		Legal assistant	
9	Reads the appeal again (thoroughly)	V	35		6	Legal assistant	
10	Decides to take the appeal into consideration	OK	30	0.5		Legal assistant	In practice: 90% of appeals are considered
11	Asks secretary to make a receipt letter	T	2			Legal assistant	
12	Types a concept receipt letter	V	3			Secretary Legal Dept.	

#	Activity	Type				Responsible	Notes
13	Checks the concept receipt letter	OK	5		7	Legal assistant	
14	Prints it on logo sheet	R	2	4		Secretary Legal Dept.	
15	Brings the receipt letter to the legal council	T	4			Secretary Legal Dept.	
16	Checks the receipt letter	OK	5	5	7	Legal council	Legal council is out of office 50% of time
17	Collects the receipt letter	T	3			Secretary Legal Dept.	
18	Puts the receipt letter in an envelope in the mailbag	T	3	0.15		Secretary Legal Dept.	
19	Daily collects the mailbag and sends it by PO	T	20	1		Mail room	
20	Receives receipt letter					Financial organization	
Total:			171 min.	15 days	24 appeals		V/W means value adding or one of the eight wastes. D = Defects, R = Rework, OK = Inspection, W = Waiting, I = Inventory, T = Transport, O = Overprocessing, and U = Insufficient use of talent

Appendix B: Project Letter

Name Kaizen team: *Application Welfare Payment*		
Group Members		
Client		Department:

"With the enactment of the Development Plan 2007, we have set ourselves the assignment of putting the customer first, leading the primary process, being an effective and efficient organization with no fatal losses, and being a fixed contact for every customer."

"We aim to increase free time by using smarter work processes, thereby ensuring that our consultants can spend more time on our primary target to lead our clients to jobs and/or social participation and achieve a better outflow and other results."

Step 1. Choice of Subject

Assignment Description:

One of the most important work tasks is to handle requests for welfare payments. Your assignment is to make this process maximally effective for our customers and maximally efficient by means of minimal action time for us, the consultant, and the welfare administration office.

Preconditions

1. Quality must meet the IGSD quality criteria (standards for integrity financial error rate < 1%).
2. Feasible and attainable within three months, using the employees currently on our payroll.
3. Using the current applications.
4. The process may not increase the client's administrative burden.

Start Date	March 5, 2007	End Date	June 5, 2007

Step 2. Targets

Cut back process lead time from the current six weeks to a maximum of two weeks.

Cut the action time consultants spend on this process by 50%.

Project Sponsor Agreement:	Date:

Appendix C: 5 × Why Diagram

Step	Actions
1	Describe the problem or the waste (what is wrong?)
2	Ask "why" to detect the probable causes
3	Register the probable cause in the columns (Why1...)
4	Validate the probable causes (preferably in practice)

When result from the validation is ...	Then ...
True	Place a √ in column V
	Go to step 5
False	Place an **X** in column V
	Go back to step 2

Step	Actions
5	Repeat steps 2 to 4 as much as needed until there is no proper answer possible

Example

Problem: Taking C-forms from Secretary to the Consultants Takes Four Days

Why1	V	Why2	V	Why3	V	Why4	V	Why5	V	Measures
Secretary sends the C-forms to the consultants too late	√	They don't know that quick response to requests is important	√	C-forms are not prioritized	√	Secretary does not know an instruction	√	There is no instruction	√	Make a visual instruction for this part of the process
								The instruction is not up to date anymore	X	
				Secretary cannot directly discriminate C-forms from other mail	√	C-forms look the same as other forms	√			Make the C-forms more distinguishable

Appendix D: Proposal for Improvement

Logo	**Proposal for Improvement**				Date:	
Name:	Workplace:				Number:	
Dept:	Subject:					
Current situation: (Description)			Proposed situation: (Description)			
(Picture, drawing, photograph)			(Picture, drawing, photograph)			
Costs:					**Approved by all:**	
Benefits:					**Implemented on (date):**	

Appendix E: Example of a 5S Audit

5S Audit

		Score[a]				
Sort	All documents and materials on desks and in drawers are used daily or weekly	1	2	3	4	5
	All documents and materials in the cabinets are used monthly	1	2	3	4	5
	All documents are filed correctly or are consistently cleared away at the correct time	1	2	3	4	5
	All filing procedures are clear and available in the location where they are used	1	2	3	4	5
	Sum First S:					
Set in order	All cabinets and stocks carry labels indicating place and item	1	2	3	4	5
	All documents and stocks have an owner or administrator	1	2	3	4	5
	Every authorized person can find office equipment within 30 seconds	1	2	3	4	5
	Every authorized person can find any document within 30 seconds	1	2	3	4	5
	Sum Second S:					
Shine	People looking for frequently used objects always find what they need	1	2	3	4	5
	Everybody knows how to clear away unnecessary objects	1	2	3	4	5
	Employees themselves keep work spaces and floors organized and free of clutter following set rules	1	2	3	4	5
	At the end of the day, all desks and work tables are empty	1	2	3	4	5
	Sum Third S:					

5S Audit (continued)

		Score[a]				
Standardize	All standards have been clearly set out and posted and are frequently used	1	2	3	4	5
	Standards are frequently evaluated and revised	1	2	3	4	5
	Designated persons are responsible for cleaning and clearing operations	1	2	3	4	5
	The progress of the primary processes is visible at a single glance	1	2	3	4	5
	Sum Fourth S:					
Sustain	Stocks and deviation from stocks are visible at a single glance (within 30 sec.)	1	2	3	4	5
	There are no documents, maps, office supplies on the floors or cabinets	1	2	3	4	5
	Suggestions for improvement are drawn up regularly; responses are prompt, within one week.	1	2	3	4	5
	Everybody always sticks to agreements on workplace organization	1	2	3	4	5
	Sum Fifth S:					
[a] Score: 1 = We constantly deviate; 5 = Flawless, no deviations ever.	Sum of all Ss					

Bibliography

Aardema, H. and A. Korsten. September 2005. *De Staat van de Gemeente*. The Hague, The Netherlands: Vereniging van GemeenteSecretarissen.

AbvaKabo FNV. 2005. http://www.abvakabofnv.nl/docs/aaneen/Uitslag_Geluksonderzoek_aaneen_nov05.pdf.

Allen, D. 2001. *Getting things done, The art of stress-free productivity*. Middlesex, U.K.: Viking Penguin.

Berg, C.F. van den, T.P.S. Steen, F.M. van der Meer, et al. 2005. *Modernizing government in other countries: International comparison of change processes in central government*. The Hague, The Netherlands: Ministry of the Interior and Kingdom Relations.

Berry, L. 1999. *Discovering the soul of service: The nine drivers of sustainable business success*, New York: The Free Press.

Binary Objects GmbH. 2010. Web site Burgerhaushalt Lichtenberg (Council of Berlin): http://www.buergerhaushalt-lichtenberg.de/ (accessed March 4, 2010).

Buddingh, H. and B. Rijlaarsdam. December 2010. *Nieuwe semocratie komt van de wijkbewoners zelf* (*New democracy comes from the residents themselves*). The Netherlands: Rotterdam, NRC Handelsblad.

Fabrizio, Th. A. and D. Tapping. 2006. *5S for the office, Organizing the workplace to eliminate waste*. New York: Productivity Press.

Federale Overheidsdienst Belgie, Personeel en Organisatie. April 2005. *Verbeterprojecten BPR; Instrument bij de modernisering van de federale vverheid (Improvement projects BPR; Instrument for the modernization of the federal government)*. Brussels, Belgium: FOD Personeel en Organisatie.

Hicks, B.J. August 2007. Lean information management: Understanding and eliminating waste. *International Journal of Information Management*, 27 (4): 233–249.

Hines, P., A. Martins, and J. Beale. February 2008. Testing the boundaries of lean thinking: Observations from the legal public sector. *Public money and management* 28 (1): 35–40.

Iowa Department of Management, Office of Lean Enterprise: http://lean.iowa.gov/ (accessed February 2010).

Kooij, M. van der. December 2007. Een beetje meer ertrouwen (A little more confidence). *Binnenlands Bestuur Week* 52 (52): 40–41.

Local Government Association. November 2009. Delivering more for less: Maximizing value in the public sector. London: LGA.

Moore, M.H. September 1994. Public value as the focus of strategy. *Australian Journal of Public Administration* 53 (3): 296–303.

Peters, Th. January 2007. Rechtvaardige regels moet je keihard toepassen. *Intermediair* 3: 35–39.

Radnor, Z. and P. Walley. February 2008. Learning to walk before we try to run: Adapting Lean for the public sector. *Public Money and Management* 28 (1): 13–20.

Seddon, J. 2008. *Systems thinking in the public sector*. Axminster, U.K.: Triarchy Press.

Swiss, J.E. July/August 1992. Adapting TQM to government. *Public Administration Review* 52 (4): 356–358.

Teeuwen, B. January 2010. *5S Werkplekorganisatie*. Gouda, The Netherlands: Yokoten.

Teeuwen, B. May 2008. *Procesgericht verbeteren in de publieke sector. Praktisch verbetermanagement voor publieke organisaties*. Driebergen, The Netherlands: WagenaarHoes.

United Kingdom Parliament. June 2009. *Putting the frontline first: Smarter government*. London: The Stationary Office.

Vandendriessche, F. 2008. *Leading without commanding*. Paris: Groupe Eyrolles.

Vandendriessche, F. September 2008. Leading without authority. *Business Digest* 188: 3–5.

Venegas, C. 2007. *Flow in the office: Implementing and sustaining Lean improvements*. New York: Productivity Press.

Westerloo, G. van. December 2007. Ambtelijke logica (Official logic). *Binnenlands Bestuur Week* 52: 36–39.

Wilcke, E., et al. May 2007. *Het geluk van werkend Nederland 2007*. Gravenhage, The Netherlands: Motivaction/Randstad Nederland.

Womack, J.P. and D.T. Jones. 1996. *Lean thinking*. New York: Free Press.

Index

About the Author

Bert Teeuwen has more than ten years of experience in coaching organizations in the Lean philosophy and in implementing improvement programs such as Lean, Six Sigma, and TPM. Teeuwen has worked in the profit sector in such organizations as Philips, Heineken, and Sabic; and in the public sector for municipal governments, counties, and federal departments.

He originally trained as a food technologist and process engineer, and his career gave him the necessary experience in the management of large operational departments in organizations. For his consultancy practice, he linked experience and pragmatics of operational management to the philosophy and tools of improvement programs.

Processes continue to fascinate Teeuwen in his consultancy practice. He has the skills and tools to make many organizations run like a well-oiled machine. Utilizing his specialization in process improvement, Teeuwen works with his clients to identify any remaining redundancies within their processes. He guides them toward a new organization, one that will perform optimally once again. He guides organizations not just in consultancy courses, but he also enjoys giving training courses in this field, or just performing a quality improvement audit. His special sense of humor is highly contagious and helps smooth the often rocky road to improvement. He can be contacted at: bertteeuwen@yokoten.nl.